DIRECTORY OF CHIEF MINISTERS OF INDIA
(1947 to 2007)

BY THE SAME AUTHOR

1. Contemporary Approach to School Library (1982)
2. Rajiv Gandhi : An Annotated Bibliography (1983)
3. Health Science Publications from India : A Guide 1947-1982 (1985)
4. Encyclopedia of Sports (1999)
5. Encyclopedia of Women in Sports (2000)
6. Governors of India including Lt. Governors (2007)
7. Services Chiefs of India : 1947-2007

DIRECTORY OF CHIEF MINISTERS OF INDIA
(1947 to 2007)

Satinder Sharma
Indra Sharma

RELIANCE PUBLISHING HOUSE
NEW DELHI (INDIA)

Cataloging in Publication Data--DK
Courtesy: D.K. Agencies (P) Ltd. <docinfo@dkagencies.com>

Sharma, Satinder, 1940-
Directory of chief ministers of India, 1947-2005
/ Satinder Sharma, Indra Sharma.
xii, 183 p.
Includes index.
ISBN 81-7510-181-4

1. Cabinet officers--India--Directories.
2. Politicians--India--Directories. 3. India
--Politics and government--1947-
--Directories. I. Title.

DDC 352.293 025 54 21

First Published **2008**

ISBN : 81-7510-181-4

Pric

Price charged
is inclusive of
delivery

Published by
Dr. S.K. Bhatia
(Life Member Common Cause, HWF, ILA & INSA Lions Clubs Int.)
for **RELIANCE PUBLISHING HOUSE**
3026/7H, Ranjit Nagar, New Delhi-110 008
Ph. 25847377 / 25842605

Composed by
Elegant Printographics
319, R. G. Complex, IIIrd Floor,
Sector-14, Rohini, Delhi-110085.
Ph. : 20514000

Printed by :

CONTENTS

Preface

After the Independence of India on 15 August 1947. India had been busy in Framing the Indian constitution and for that purpose constitution Assembly was constituted which included Prominent Political leaders like Mahatama Gandhi, Pandit Jawaharlal Nehru, Dr. Rajendera Prasad, Sardar Patel, Dr. B.R. Ambedkar, and learned persons in various fields. The constitution Assembly was Presided over by Dr. Rajendra Prasad, Members of Minority community Christians, Muslims, Sikhs and Parsis were included. Dr. Ambedkar was the chairman of the Drafting committee of the constitution. This constitution was finally adopted in 1951 and Dr. Rajendra Prasad was the First President of Indian Republic. The Structure of the constitution was Federal. The provinces were supposed to have Legislative Assembly and Legislative council. This constitution guaranteed the strong center with certain subjects like Defence, Foreign Policy, Customs, Excise and Finance etc., under its control subject like Law and order, Education and Local Taxes etc were under states and chief ministers as head of their respective states. Their position and power in the states were same as that of Prime Minister in the country but their Jurisdiction remained the concerned state.

Council of Ministers and Chief Minister

The constitution provides for a council of ministers with chief minister as its head. The Governor appoints the chief minister and approves the council of ministers. They should be the members of the Legislature of the state suggested by chief minister. If a non-member is appointed as minister he/she has to become the member of the state Legislature within six months. The council of ministers is responsible to the Legislature collectively and individually. They remain in office for five years or till they enjoy the confidence of the Legislature. The chief minister presides over the meetings of the cabinet.

Chief minister being the most important person in the state is the focus of this book. There is no such book so far which gives the biographical profiles of the chief ministers of India since independence. So we thought upon to produce a reference tool in the form of this book which provides brief life sketches of the chief ministers of India.

We hope this book will fill up the gap and serve as a reference tool for the scholars and Inquisitive readers in general. We feel highly obliged to Dr. S. K. Bhatia of Reliance Publishing House. Assam, Bihar, Himachal, Kerala, Punjab, Manipur, Maharashtra Information centers for their valuable help and Smt. Santosh Devi of Haryana House and Sheela rani Shukla of Chattisgarh for their co-operation in compilation. We express regret for any error gone undetected or omission, if any.

We feel highly obliged to the Director, Staff of Nehru Memorial Museum and Library for their valuable co-operation.

F-239, Sawan Cottage,
Pandav Nagar,
Delhi-110091
India

Satinder Sharma.
Indra Sharma.

LIST OF PHOTOGRAPHS

LIST OF ABBREVIATIONS USED

AD	=	Akali Dal
AGP	=	Assam Gana Parishad
AIADMK	=	All India Anna Dravida Munnetra Kazhagam
AICC	=	All India Congress Committee
AIR	=	All India Radio
APCC	=	Andhra Pradesh Congress Committee
APHLC	=	All Party Hill Leaders Conference
Bar-at-Law	=	Barrister-at-Law
BBS	=	Bharat Sewak Samaj
BJP	=	Bhartiya Janta Party
BKD	=	Bhartiya Kranti Dal
BLD	=	Bhartiya Lok Dal
BSP	=	Bahujan Samaj Party
CDM	=	Civil Disobedience Movement
CMP	=	Common Minimum Programme
CPI	=	Communist Party of India
CPI(M)	=	Communist Party of India (Marxist)
DCC	=	District Congress Committee
DMK	=	Dravida Munnetra Kazhagam
ESCAP	=	Economic and Social Council for Asia and Pacific
FB	=	Forward Block
FCA	=	Food Corporation of India
FICCI	=	Federation of Indian Chambers of Commerce and Industry
GOI	=	Government of India
HP	=	Himachal Pradesh
IAS	=	Indian Administrative Service
ICFTU	=	International Confederation of Free Trade Unions
ICS	=	Indian Civil Service
Ind	=	Independent
IIPA	=	Indian Institute of Public Administration
INTUC	=	Indian National Trade Union Congress
IPS	=	Indian Police Service
J&K	=	Jammu and Kashmir

JMM	=	Jharkhand Mukti Morcha
KC	=	Kerala Congress
KLA	=	Karnataka Legislative Assembly
LD	=	Lok Dal
LLB	=	Bachelor of Law
LLM	=	Master of Law
MLA	=	Member of Legislative Assembly
MLC	=	Member Legislative Council
MNF	=	Mizo National Front
MP	=	Member of Parliament
MPCC	=	Madhya Pradesh Congress Committee
NC	=	National Conference
NDA	=	National Democratic Alliance
NDP	=	National Democratic Party
NNDP	=	Naga National Democratic Party
NPCC	=	Naga Pradesh Congress Committee
NWFP	=	North West Frontier Province
PCA	=	Public Accounts Committee
PDP	=	People's Democratic Party
PPCC	=	Punjab Pradesh Congress Committee
PSP	=	Praja Socialist Party
RJD	=	Rashtriya Janata Dal
RKP	=	Rashtriya Kranti Party
RSP	=	Revolutionary Socialist Party
SP	=	Samata Party
TD	=	Telugu Desham
TN	=	Tamil Nadu
TNA	=	Tamil Nadu Assembly
UK	=	United Kingdom
UN	=	United Nations
UNCTAD	=	United Nation's Conference on Trade and Development
UPA	=	United Progressive Alliance
UP	=	Uttar Pradesh
USA	=	United States of America

CHIEF MINISTERS OF ANDHRA PRADESH

S. No.	*Name*	*Term of Office*
ANDHRA STATE		
1.	Tanguturi Prakasham	01.10.1953 to 15.11.1954
	President's Rule	15.11.1954 to 28.03.1955
2.	Bezawada Gopala Reddy	28.03.1955 to 31.01.1956
HYDERABAD SATE		
1.	Burgula Ramakrishna Rao	06.03.1952 to 31.10.1956
ANDHRA PRADESH STATE		
1.	Neelam Sanjeeva Reddy	01.11.1956 to 10.01.1960
2.	Damaodaram Sanjivayya.	11.01.1960 to 11.03.1962
3.	Neelam Sanjeeva Reddy	12.03.1962 to 28.02.1964
4.	Kasu Brahmananda Reddy	29.02.1964 to 29.09.1971
5.	P.V. Narasimha Rao President rules	30.09.1971 to 18.01.1973 18.01.1973 to 10.12.1973
6.	Jalagam Vengal Rao	11.12.1973 to 05.03.1978
7.	Marri Chenna reddy	06.03.1978 to 10.10.1980
8.	Anjaiah Tanaguturi	11.10.1980 to 24.02.1982
9.	B. Venkatram reddy	24.02.1982 to 20.09.1982
10.	K. Vijaybhaskar Reddy	20.09.1982 to 08.01.1983
11.	N.T. Rama Rao	09.01.1983 to 16.08.1984
12.	Bhaskara Rao Nadendla	16.08.1984 to 15.09.1984
13.	N.T. Rama Rao Care-taker Government	16.09.1984 to 22.11.1984 22.11.1984 to 08.03.1985
14.	N.T. Rama Rao	09.03.1985 to 02.12.1989
15.	Marri Chenna Reddy	03.12.1989 to 17.12.1990
16.	N. Janardhan Reddy	17.12.1990 to 08.10.1992
17.	K. Vijayabhaskar Reddy	09.10.1992 to 12.12.1994
18.	N.T. Rama Rao	12.12.1994 to 31.08.1995
19.	N. Chandrababu Naidu	01.09.1995 to 11.10.1995
20.	N. Chadrababu Naidu	11.10.1999 to 13.05.2004
21.	Y.S. Raja Shekhara	14.05.2004 to till date

ANDHRA PRADESH

ANJAIAH TANGUTURI
Son of M.K.T. Pappy Reddy & Maniky-amma.
Bhanur Village, Medak District (AP). 1929-18 October, 1986
Matric
Minister of state for Labour (Independent charge).

08 June – 11 October 1980, again 31 December 1984 –19 January 1986. He was General Secretary, Congress (I) since January 1986. Elected to Rajya Sabha 1978. Chief Minister of Andhra Pradesh 1980-82.

Helped in the approval of Palekar award for the Working Journalists and non Journalists, toured USSR & Japan under UNESCO plan.

- 12/3 R.T. Barkat Pura, Hyderabad – 500 027.

BEZWADA GOPALA REDDY
Son of B. Pattabhi Rami Reddi
05 August 1907-08 March, 1997, Nellore A.P.
Viswa Bharati, Shantiniketan

Married B. Lakshmikanth Amma. Indian Politician elected to Madras Assembly 1937. Member 1937-46. Minister of Local Government. Madras Government 1937-39. Minister of Finance 1947, Pro-chancellor, A.P. University 1951-57.Elected to Rajya Sabha 1958-60, to Lok Sabha 1962 Deputy Leader Congress Party 1965-71, Head of the United Congress Legislative Party, A.P. Assembly 1955. Chief Minister A.P. 1955-56, Home Minister 1956. Finance Minister 1957, Governor of Uttar Pradesh 1967-72.

BHASKARA RAO NADENDLA
Son of Pitchaiah and Venkayamma.
Guntur, 01 July 1935.
B.A., L.L.B., L.S.G.D.

Has practiced for 16 years at High court : General Secretary APCC (I) 78 elected to Assembly and was minister in Dr. Chenna Reddy, Anjiah and NTR's cabinet; Chief Minister for a month, August 1984 to 15 September, 1984.

- 245, Jubilee Hills, Hyderabad.

BHAVANAM VENKATARAMA REDDY

Bhavanam venkatarama sworn in as chief minister of Andhra Pradesh on 24 February 1982.

BURGULA RAMAKRISHNA RAO

He was Chief Minister of Hyderabad State from 06.03.1952 to 31.10.1956

CHANDRABABU NAIDU

Naravaripally, Dist. Chittor (A.P.), 20 April 1950.

M.A. (Economics)

The Andhra Pradesh Chief Minister was declared the "South Asian of the year 1994" by the American news magazine Time. The lead article under the column "The Sun continental Drift" called Mr. Chandrababu Naidu as the sub-continent's most visionary Politicians, saying that in just five years, he has turned an impoverished rural back water into India's new information Technology Lab.

Chief Minister since September 1995 elected to Legislative Assembly, 78, 89, 94, 99. Vice-President A.P. Youth Congress (I). Director A.P. Small Industries Development Corporation. Minister of States, Archives and cinematography in T.Anjaiah's Cabinet inducted as Finance and Revenue Minister in the Cabinet of N.T. Rama Rao. He is Chief Minister Andhra Pradesh since September 1995-1999. IT Man of the Year 1999 by Computer World. "The Business Person of the Year"1998 by Economic Times. 1999 to 13.05.2004

Chief Minister's Secretariate, Hyderabad.

DAMODRAM SANJIVAYYA

Anantapur; February 14, 1921.

B.A., B.L. from Madras Law college.

Enrolled as an Advocate, 1950 joined The congress and was elected to parliament from the Madras Legislature as a congress nominee, elected M.L.A. (Madras) from Kurnool Reserved constituency as a congress candicate in the general elections,

1952. Minister of Co-operation and Housing, Govt of Madras, 1952-54; Minister for Local Administration and Labour, Andhra Pradesh, till January 1960. Chief Minister Govt. of Andhra Pradesh since January 1960.

JALAGAM VENGAL RAO
Son of Venkata Rao.
Sopeur (Srikakulam Distt. AP) 4 May 1922.
Matriculate

Member Andhra Pradesh Legislative Assembly 1962-78. Minister of Home Affairs, Government of Andhra Pradesh 1969-71, for industries 1972-73, Chief Minister of Andhra Pradesh 1973-78. Minister for Industries, Govt. of India 1986-89. Chairman Zilla Parishad, 1959-64; elected to Lok Sabha 1989.
- Dwarkapuri Colony, Hyderabad

K. VIJAYA BHASKARA REDDY
Son of K. Pedda Nagi Reddy.
Laddagiri, Kurnool District (AP).
16 August, 1920-27 September, 1992.
B.A. L.L.B.

Politician Congress (I) M.P. Kurnool A.P. Agriculturist. Practicing Lawyer till 1955. Minister Govt. of A.P. 1967-71 was also briefly Chief Minister of Andhra Pradesh, Chairman Zilla Prishad Kurnool 1959 & 1964-67. Member Andhra Pradesh Assembly 1955-62 & Council 1967-72. Member, Chairman Andhra Pradesh Sports Council 1968-70. He was Cabinet Minister without Portfolio – 29 January – 02 February 1983.

Industry & Company Affairs – 04 November – 31 December 1984. Law Justice & Company Affairs – 21 June 1991 – 08 October 1992. Chief Minister AP, September 1982 – January 83 and Chief Minister 1992-94. Minister of shipping & Transport 1983-1984, Minister of Law and Justice & Company Affairs 1991 Sept. 1992.
- 7-1-121/4, Ameerpet, Hyderabad.
- Laddagiri, Dist. Kurnool (AP).

KASU BRAKMMANANDA REDDY
Son of Kasu Ventaka Krishna Reddy.
Chirumamilla Village, Guntur District. (Andhra Pradesh)
28 July 1909-20 May, 1994.
B.A., L.L.B

Member, A.I.C.C. Andhra University Senate, imprisoned 1941 and detained 1942. President Guntur District Board, 1946. Member Madras Assembly 1946-52. General Secretary Andhra Pradesh Congress Committee from march 19551 Finance Minister 1960-62. Chief Minister, Andhra Pradesh, since February 29, 1964-71.

Cabinet Minister for Communications – 11 January – 10 October 1974.

Home Affairs – 10 October 1974 – 24 March 1977.

Agriculture & Irrigation – 03 February – 24 March 1977.

Industry – 30 July – 27 November 1979. President Indian National Congress 1977-78 (resigned). Member Lok Sabha for Narasaropet.Member Rajya-Sabha 1974-77. He was Governor of Maharashtra since February 1988.

Dr. MARRI CHENNA REDDY
Son of M. Lakshma Reddy.
Sirpur Village, Hyderabad District (Andhra Pradesh)
13 January 1919-02 December, 1996
M.B.B.S.

Politician. Chief Minister of Andhra Pradesh 1978-80. Member Hyderabad Assembly 1952-67. Cabinet Minister for Steel, Mines & Metals – 16 March 1967-27 April 1968. Governor U.P. 1974-77. Resigned as Governor in October 1977 to enter active Politics. Second time Chief Minister 03.12.1989 to 17.12.1990

N. JANARDHANA REDDY
Son of N. Subbaranu& Seshamma.
Vakadu Village (District Nellore, AP) 20 February 1935.
B.A. B.Ed.

Former Andhra Pradesh Chief Minister was appointed chairman of Parliament's Public Accounts committee (PCA) on March 15, 2002. Chief Minister of AP, 1990-92 was actively

associated with students union congress, youth movements, eleted to Rajya Sabha 1972 President, APCC
- Village & P.O. Vakadu, Dist. Nellore (AP).

N.T. RAMARAO
Son of Laxmiah & Venkata - Ramamma
Nimmakuru (AP) – 28 May 1923 to 18 January, 1996
B.A.

Chief Minister of Andhra Pradesh since September 1984 for second term. Joined Madras Service Commission in 1974 as sub-Registrar but resigned in three weeks & took to films. Worked in October 1981. Launched Telugu Desam Party in March 1982; emerged victorious in AP Assembly elections, January 1983 and became Chief Minister Formulated 15 Point Programme for all round development of Andhra Pradesh was asked to resign in August 1984 by the Governor of AP, but was sworn in again as Chief Minister in September 1984. Enacted male and female roles in Telugu dramas during students. Entered films, 1948 and has enacted roles in more than 300 films on Mythological, Historical, Folklore and Social themes attaining fame and popularity.

He was Chief Minister of Andhra Pradesh:-
(1) 09.01.1983 to 16.08.1983,
(2) 16.09.1984 to 22.11.1984,
(3) 09.03.1985 to 02.12.1989,
(4) 12.12.1994 to 31.08.1995

Award "Padmashri" 1968.

NEELAM SANJEEVA REDDY
Son of Chinnappa Reddy.
Ilur, Anantpur District (Andhra Pradesh)
19 May, 1913-1 June, 1996
Intermediate.

President of India 1977-82. Secretary Andhra PCC 1936-46. Deputy Chief Minister Andhra 1953 and 1955-56.

Chief Minister 1956-60 and 1962-64. Cabinet Minister for Steel & Mines – 09 June 1964-24 January 1966.

Transport, Aviation, shipping & Tourism – 24 January 1966-12 March 1967. Freedom Fighter. President Indian National Congress 1960-62. Member Lok Sabha from Hindupur, Andhra Pradesh and Speaker of Lok Sabha 1967-69.

Speaker Lok Sabha March-July1977, President of India 25.07.1977 to 25.07.1982

P.V. NARASIMHA RAO

Son of P.Ranga Rao

Karimnagar District (A.P.) 28 June, 1921–24 December, 2004.

B.Sc. L.L.B., Sahitya Ratna.

Cabinet Minister of External Affairs – 14 January 1980 – 19 July 1984. Defence.

Home Affairs 19 July 1984 – 31 December 1984.

Human Resource Development – 25 September 1985 – 25 June 1988.

Again H.R.D. 17 January – 16 May 1996.

Prime Minister of India, 1991 – 1996. Formerly, Chief Minister (Andhra Pradesh) 1971-73, convicted in (JMM) MP's bribery case in September 2000. President Andhra Pradesh congress committee 1956, member Assembly 1955 – 77. General Secretary Indian National Congress 1974-77, member Lok Sabha 1977-79, re-elected 1980, 84, 89, took part in Vandamatram movement in former Hyderabad State.

TANGUTURI PRAKASAM

Ongole Taluk, Andhra Pradesh. 1876.

B.A., Bar – at – Law.

Entered municipal Politics early in Life was elected municipal chairman. Set up Practice at Madras. Chief Minister Andhra state since October 1953 to November, 1954.

Y.S. RAJASEKHARA

His father, an influential Political Figure, was murdedred by rivals in 1998, Mother served as Panchayat President. Y.S.R's mother Jayamma reacted to the landslide victory of Congress. She said, "Pulivendula is a dry area. He will now be able to get

water for the constituency.
Born to Protestant Parents in 1949
M.B.B.S.

President of Students Union in Medical College, he joined Politics after a short stint as a doctor. Become M.L.A at 28 in 1978. Deeply inspired by Indira Gandhi in her socialist phase.

Y.S. Raja Sekhara became P.C.C. President when he was 34 and has struggled to get to Power since then. Two close brushes with power, in 1994 and 1999 when he almost became Chief Minister, left him lchastened. Then, when all seemed to going Naidu's way, this guy suddenly got up and went on a 1,500 KM walked out on his Parched State.

"Peoples expectation are very high. It's almost Scary, but I'll do my best", he said. "Irrigation and agriculture are the most important subject to that TDP neglected," he says. "We'll focus on industrial development'. Will big businesses, much favoured by Naidu, get the brush-off? "We won't change any Policy that has the people's mandate,"replies YSR.
He became Chief Minister of Andhra Pradesh on 14.05.2004. Loves reading biographies. His favourite book is "The God Father"

CHIEF MINISTERS OF ARUNACHAL PRADESH

Sr. No.	Name	Term of Office	
1.	Prem Khandu Thungon	1975	
2.	Prem Khandu Thungon	1978	1979
3.	Toma Riba	1979	
4.	Gegong Apang	1980	
5.	Mukut Mithi	1999	Till date

ARUNACHAL PRADESH

Arunachal Pradesh became 24th States of India on February 20, 1987.

GEGONG APANG
Son of Emi Apang.
Karko Vill. (East Siang Dist. Arunachal) 10 Jan. 1947
B.A.
Chief Minister of Arunachal Pradesh since 1980. Member, Arunachal Pradesh Council, 1972-75 & first Provisional Legislative Assembly, 1975-78. Minister of Agriculture 1977, elected to first Legislative Assembly 1978. Minister, PWD Agriculture etc. 1978. Elected leader of Congress (I) Legislative Party in ALP, 1980. Founder & Chairman Boum Kakir Mission (for orphans) & Donyi Polo Vidhya Bhawan at New Itanagar 1982 elected to Assembly in 1975, 78, 80, 84, 90, 95.

Chief Minister's Residence, New Itanagar 791110.

He was sorn in on 16 October, 2004.

MUKUT MITHI
Son of Khumso Mithi.
Roing, 01 January 1954.
B.Sc.

Undertook active part in various Social activities in Dibong valley; elected to Arunachal pradesh Assembly, 1983, 84, 90, 95; Deputy Minister for Forest, 1985. Minister for Forest and PR & Tourim, 1987 for Sports 1992. for Health and Family Welfare 94 for A.H. and Veternary 1995-96, for Home 1996. Chief Minister of AP since January 1999.
- Roing, Dibang Valley, Dist. Arunachal Pradesh.

PREM KHANDU THUNGON
Son of Pema Wangdi Thungon.
Shergon Village, West kameng District (AP). 05 June 1946.
B.A.

Chief Minister of Arunachal Pradesh 1975; elected unopposed and became Chief Minister again in 1978-79, was Leader of Opposition in Arunachal Assembly, 1979 elected to Lok Sabha 1980, 84, 89, 91.

He was Deputy Minister for Supply & Rehabilitation – 08 June 1980 – 15 January 1982.

Education, Culture Social Welfare – 15 January 1982 – 31 October 1984.

Water Resources – 19 February 1993 – 09 February 1995.

- Village Shergaon, Dist. Kameng (Arunachal Pradesh).

TOMO RIBA (PPA)
Son of Late Rito Riba
1934
B.A.

General Secretary, District Council 1959-61. West Siang, Arunachal Pradesh. Chief Councillor, Arunachal Pradesh Legislative Council 1973-75. Formed People's Party of Arunachal Pradesh 1977. Chief Minister of Arunachal Pradesh, 1979. In 1996 Elected to Lok Sabha (Eleventh). 1980-89 President, Peoples Party of Arunachal Pradesh. Interested in Social Work since student days. Served as a Field Publicity Officer in the Directorate of Field Publicity, Govt. of India for five years. Joined Council of Ministers as Minister of Agriculture, Horticulture & Animal Husbandry in 1975 till 1977.

- C1/13, Lodhi Garden, New Delhi-110003

CHIEF MINISTERS OF ASSAM

S. No.	Name	Term of Office	
1.	Maulavi Saiyid Sir Mohammad Saadulla Premier	7-4-1937	19-9-1938
	Maulavi Saiyid Sir Mohammad Saadulla Premier	17-11-1939	25-12-1941
	Maulavi Saiyid Sir Mohammad Saadulla Premier	12-11-1942	10-2-1946
2.	Gopinath Bordoloi Premier	19-9-1938	17-11-1939
	Gopinath Bordoloi Premier	11-7-1946	06-08-1950
3.	Bishnu Ram Medhi	09-8-1950	27-12-1957
4.	Bimala Prosad Chabiha	28-12-1957	6-11-1970
5.	Mahendra Mohan Choudhury	6-11-1970	31-1-1972
6.	Sarat Chandra Sinha	31-1-1972	12-3-1978
7.	Golap Borbora	12-3-1978	8-9-1978
8.	Jogendra Nath Hazarika	9-9-1978	11-12-1979
9.	Smt. Syeda Anowara Taimur	6-12-1980	30-6-1981
10.	Keshab Chandra Gogoi	13-1-1982	19-3-1982
11.	Hiteswar Saikia	27-2-1983	23-12-1985
	Hiteswar Saikia	30-6-1991	22-4-1996
12.	Dr. Bhumidhar Barman	22-4-1994	14-5-1996
13.	Prafulla Kumar Mahanta	24-12-1985	27-11-1990
	Prafulla Kumar Mahanta	15-6-1996	17-5-2001
14.	Tarun Gogoi	18-5-2001	Till date

ASSAM

BIMALAPROSAD CHABIHA
Sibsagar, March 26, 1912.
Matric

Left studies when he was in I.Sc. Join the National Movement. Arrested in 1932 and jailed for six months. Elected Secretary, All India Spinners Association Assam Branch till 1942. Detained for two years as Security Prisoner during 1942 Movement. Elected M.L.A. Assam from Sibsagar West 1946. Appointed Parliamentary Secretary 1947. General Secretary, A.P.C.C.; 1950; elected President A.P.C.C. 1952; won by election from Sibsagar to became Member Lok Sabha 1953. Regional Organiser for constructive work A.I.C.C. for Eastern Zone 1952. Elected Chairman Reception Committee of the 63rd session of the Indian National Congress, resigned December 1957. Chief Minister Assam since December 1957 to 06.11.1970.

BISNU RAM MEDHI
Village of Hajo (Kamrup-Assam) April 1890.
B.Sc. (Hons.), M.Sc. B.L.

Enrolled as pleader, Gauhati Bar, 1914 and Advocate, Calcutta High Court, 1931; Joined the Non-Co-operation Movement and was imprisoned for about a year in 1921. Unanimously elected President of Assam PCC after Lahore Congress and since then continuously elected president till 1939. Member A.I.C.C.; imprisoned in 1930 and 1940 in connection with C.D. and satyagraha Movements for about two years. Popularly and Legislation, Assam, February 1946-August 1950. (1) Chief Minister, Assam : August 1950 January 1958. (2) Governor of Madras 1958-64.

- Uzan Bazar, Gauhati, Assam.

DR. BHUMIDHAR BARMAN
S/o Late Bhakat Ram Barman
01-03-1930, Rukmini Nagar, District, Dispur, Guwahati
M.B.B.S.

Medical Practitioner, Member Legislative Assembly 1967-1972, Member Legislative Assembly 1972-1978, M.L.A. & Minister 1983-1985, M.L.A. & Minister 1991-1996. Chief Minister, 22.04.1994 to 14.05.1996 M.L.A. and Minister, 2001.

Indian Nation Congress (I)

GOLAP BORBORA

He was Chief Minister of Assam from
12-03-1978 to 08-09-1978

GOPINATH BORDOLOI

1890-1950.

One of the makers of modern Assam. He was Educationist, Chief Minister of Assam twice before Independence. (i) 1938 to 1939 (ii) 1946 to 1950.

Award "Bharat Ratna, 1999."

HITESWAR SAIKIA

Son of Holadhan and Khogeswari
Assam at Boga Bagh Tea, 02 October 1954.
M.A.

Congress (I) Politician, 1) Chief Minister of Assam 1983-85 and 30-6-1991 to 22-4-1996. Minister of State for Home. Government of Assam 1972; elevated to Cabinet rank 1974. Member Assam Legislative Assembly since 1972 .He was Vice Principal Gargaon College, 1960-72.

(1) Lt. Governor of Mozoram 1986- February 1987.

(2) Governor of Mizoram 1987-89.

JOGENDRA NATH HAZARIKA

Son of Shri Golap Chandra Hazarika.
Dibrugarh, Assam-1957. Scheduled Tribe
Khangia Village, Distt. Lakhimpur.
February, 1924.
M.A., LL.B.

Married Smt. Veena Devi May, 1952. He was Member Parliamentary Delimidtation Committee, Advisory Committee for Assam, Road Communication Advisory Committee, Member Executive of the Congress Parliamentary Member Provisional Parliament (1950-52). Member, First Lok Sabha and Parliamentary Secretary to the Prime Minister (1952-57). Chief Minister of Assam 9-9-1978 – 11-12-1979.

KESHAB CHANDRA GOGOI

Shri Keshab chandra Gogoi elected leader of the congress (1) legislature Party in Assam and sworn in as chief Minister of Assam on 13 January 1982 to 19 March, 1982. Presidents rule revoked. The 64-day old congress (2) Ministry in Assam headed by K.C. Gogoi resigns. on 18 March 1982

MAHENDRA MOHAN CHODHURY

Nagaon, Assam. 12 April 1908

B.A., L.L.B. (Gauhati)

Participated in Freedom struggle, elected M.A.L. 1946. Parliamentary Secretary, 1947; subsequently became Deputy Minister & Cabinet Minister Assam 1950-55. General Secretary, A.I.C.C., 1956-57; elected to Rajya Sabha 1956. Chief Minister, Assam State since November 1970-1972. President Assam Pradesh Congress Committee 1955-56.

Publications : (1) Life of Mahatma Gandhi, (2) Life and Philosophy of Acharya Vinoba Bhave. Governor of Punjab 1973-77.

MAULAVI SAIYID SIR MOHAMMAD SAUDULLA

He was premier of Assam

1. 07-104-1937 to 19-09-1938
2. 17-11-1939 to 25-12-1941 and
3. 12-11-1942 to 10-02-1946

PRAFULLA KUMAR MAHANTA

Son of Deva Kanta & Lakshmi Prava (Kaliabore; Nagaon).

Rupnarayan Satra (Kaliabore; Nagaon), Assam. 30 December 1952. Married Jayasree Goswami.

B.Sc. L.L.B.

Politician. Chief Minister of Assam, December 1985-1990. President Assam Gana Parishad, since 1985-1990. All Assam Students union 1979-85. Elected to the Assam Legislative Assembly from Nowong and Kaliabar constituencies December 1985. Signed Assam accord with the Govt. of India August 1985. Ending the agitation against the inflex of foreigners into Assam. Youngest elected head of the state government in the world. Founder Assam Gana Parishad (regional political party, 1985. Again Chief Minister 1996-2001.

- (1) The Secretariat, Dispur 781005, Assam.
- (2) Rupnarayan Satra, Kalibore District Nagaon (Assam)

SARAT CHANDRA SINHA

Shri Sarat Chandra Sinha was Chief Minister of Assam State from 31-1-1972 to 12-3-1978.

SYEDA ANWARA TAIMUR (Smt.)

The Leader of the congress (1) Legislature party in Assam and the former Chief Minister 6-12-1980 – 30-6-1981. Syeda Anwara Taimur resigns from the Party leadership on 9 January 1982.

TARUN GOGOI

Rangajan Tea Estate in Jorhat District.April 01, 1936

B.A., L.L.B. (Guwahati University)

Started his career as a lawyer and simultaneously engaged himself in socio-political activities. Since student-life, qualities of leadership were evident in him when he held important positions in Students' Unions including Commandership of Students' Volunteer Corps.

In 1968, he was elected as a member of Jorhat Municipal Board, By this time, he established his gutts as a capable youth leader of Assam. Late Prime Minister Indira Gandhi spotted his promising young talent and in 1971 entrusted him with the responsibility of organizing the youth community of the State. In that year itself i.e. 1971, Shri Gogoi was elected to the Fifth Lok

Sabha. In 1976, he became the joint Secretary of All India Congress Committee. He was re-elected to the Sixth Lok Sabha in 1977. Then again, he was re-elected to the Sevent Lok Sabha in 1983. He became the General Secretary of All India Congress Committee in 1985. During 1986-90, he served as the President of Assam Pradesh Congress (I) Committee.

For the fourth time, he was elected to the 10th Lok Sabha in 1991. During that time, he was also the Vice President, APCC(I).

During 1991-93, he was the Union Minister of Food (Independent Charge). From 1993-95, he held the portfolio of Food Processing Industry in the Union Minister of state (Independent Charge).

During 1996-98, he was elected Member of Assam Legislative Assembly from Margherita Constituency. He was elected as a Member of Parliament for the fifth time in 1998 to Twelfth Lok Sabha. Again in 1999, Shri Gogoi was re-elected to the Thirteenth Lok Sabha. This is his sixth tenure as a Memebr of Parliament. Since 1966, he has been the President of the Assam Pradesh Congress Committee.

Shri Gogoi is a widely – traveled man. His favourite pastime is reading and gardening. He loves sports too. He married Smt. Dolly Gogoi in 1972 and they are blessed with a son and a daughter.

Shri Gogoi, during his colourful career, also adored important positions as Director, Vayudoot, Member, Bar Council of Assam and Chairman, Assam Small Industries Development Corporation.

Shri Gogoi become Chief Minister of Assam on 19th May, 2001 to till date.

CHIEF MINISTERS OF BIHAR

S. No.	Name	Term of Office	
1.	Dr. Krishan Singh	2-4-1946	31-1-1961
2.	Deep Narayan Singh	1-2-1961	18-2-1961
3.	Binodanand Jha	18-2-1961	2-10-1963
4.	Krishna Ballabh Sahay	2-10-1963	5-3-1967
5.	Mahamaya Prasad Sinha	5-3-1967	28-1-1968
6.	Satish Prasad Singh	28-1-1968	1-2-1968
7.	B.P. Mandal	1-2-1968	22-3-1968
8.	Bhola Paswan Shastri	22-3-1968	29-6-1968
	President's Rule	29-6-1968	26-2-1969
9.	Sardar Harihar Singh	26-2-1969	22-6-1969
10.	Bhola Paswan Shastri	22-6-1969	4-7-1969
	President's Rule	4-7-1969	16-2-1970
11.	Daroga Prasad Rai	16-2-1970	22-12-1970
12.	Karpoori Thakur	22-12-1970	2-6-1971
13.	Bhola Paswan Shastri	2-6-1971	9-1-1972
	President's Rule	9-1-1972	9-3-1972
14.	Kedar Panday	9-3-1972	2-7-1973
15.	Abdul Ghafoor	2-7-1973	11-4-1975
16.	Dr. Jagannath Mishra	11-4-1975	30-4-1977
	President's Rule	30-4-1977	24-6-1977
17.	Karpoori Thakur	24-6-1977	21-4-1978
18.	Ram Sundar Dass	21-4-1978	17-2-1980
	President's Rule	17-2-1980	8-6-1980
19.	Dr. Jagnnath Mishra	8-6-1980	14-8-1983
20.	Chander Shekhar Singh	14-8-1983	12-3-1985
21.	Bindeshwari Dubey	12-3-1985	13-2-1988
22.	Bhagwat Jha Azad	14-2-1988	11-3-1989
23.	Satyendra Narayan Sinha	11-3-1989	6-12-1989
24.	Dr. Jagnnath Mishra	6-12-1989	10-3-1990
25.	Laloo Prasad Yadav	10-3-1990	10-7-1997
26.	Smt. Rabri Devi	10-7-1997	Feb 2005
27.	President's Rule	Feb. 2005	24-11-2005
28.	Nitish Kumar	24-11-2005	Till Date

BIHAR

ABDUL GHAFOOR
Son of Basir Ali
Sariya Akhtiyan (Distt. Gopalganj) Bihar, 1918
M.A. L.L.B. Congress (I)

He was associated with Forward Block, Member Bihar Legislative Assembly 1952-66, 1968-84. Lok Sabha 1984-89, 1991 was Deputy Minister and Chief Minister of Bihar 1973 to 75 was Chairman Bihar Legislative Council, 1967.

Minister for Works & Housing GOI, 1984.

B.P. MANDAL
Son of Late Babu Rasbehari Lal Mandal.
Varanasi; August 25. 1918 – 13 April 1982.
B.A. (Janata).

Agriculturist, associated with congress Samyukta socialist Party and Shoshit Dal; Member, District Board, Member, Bihar Legislative Assembly, 1952-57 and 1962-67, (ii) Bihar Legislative council, 1968, resigned membership of Bihar Legislative council in 1968; Member, Bihar Legislative Assembly 1972-75, Minister of Health, Government of Bihar 1967 and chief Minister of Bihar 1968 to 22.03.1968; Member Fourth Lok Sabha, 1967-70.

BHAGWAT JHA AZAD
Son of J.L. Jha
Kasha Village, Santhal Pargana District (Bihar).
28 November, 1922
B.A. (Hons.) M.A. B.L.

Minister of State of Education – 18 Mar, 1967-14 Feb, 1969.
Food & Civil Supplied (Independent Charge)

15 February 1983-31 October 1984, again 04 November –31 December 1984 Member Lok Sabha 1952, 1957, 1962-67, 1967-70, 1971-77, and 1980.

Chief Minister of Bihar February 1988-89.

- Bhikanpurm Bhagalpur (Bihar) Kasba Village, Dudhichak P.O. Santhal Paranas District (Bihar).

BHOLA PASWAN SHASTRI
Bairgachhi Village (Purnea Distt., Bihar) 1914.
Shastri, Kashi Vidyapith.

He was Chairman, Scheduled Castes & Scheduled Tribes Commission since August 1978. Joined Non-Co-operation movement while in school. Courted imprisonment several times. Elected to Assembly 1946, Parliamentary Secretary to Minister for Local self Govt. 1952, Cabinet Minister 1952-63, resigned from Congress and formed Lok Tantric Dal 68, Chief Minister, Bihar 1968 and became Chief Minister again 1971-72; elected to Rajya Sabha 1972. Minister for works and Housing, GOI 1973-74.

BINDESHWARI DUBEY
Son of Sheo Naresh Dubey
Mahuaon Village, Bhojpur District (Bihar). Died 20 Jan, 1993
Diploma in Engineering.

He was chief Minister, Government of Bihar 1985-88. Union Minister of Law & Justice from February 1988 to June 1988. Labour 1988-89, elected to Rajya Sabha in April, 1988.

BINODANAND JHA
Bihar, 1900.
Calcutta.

Entered freedom movement 1917, jailed five times during political activities; elected commissioner, Deoghar Municipality; elected M.L.A., Bihar 1936. Parliamentary Secretary 1937-39, Minister for L.S.G. and Public Health Bihar 1946. Chief Minister Bihar, 1961-63; resigned under the "Kamaraj Plan" August 1963; has been taking active interest in Trade Union Movement.

CHANDER SHEKHAR SINGH

He was Chief Minister of Bihar 14-8-1983 to 13-3-1985.

DAROGA PRASAD RAI

Shri Daroga Prasad Rai was Chief Minister of Bihar for few month 16-2-1970 to 22-12-1970

DEEP NARAYAN SINGH

Shri Deep Narayan Singh was Chief Minister of Bihar for few days e.g. from 1-2-1961 to 18-2-1961.

Dr. JAGANNATH MISHRA

Son of Rabiandan Mishra

Basanpatti (Distt. Saharsa Bihar) 24 June 1937.

B.A. (Hons.), M.A., Ph.D.

He was Lecturer, Reader and later Prof. of Bihar University, Participated in Bhoodan Movement, 1953-60; member Senate and Syndicate Bihar University, 1966, was Leader of opposition in Assembly, 1977-80, 1990-94. Cabinet Minister for Rural Areas & Employment – 10 June 1955-16 May, 1996.

Agriculture 18 January – 16 May 1996.

Chief Minister of Bihar 1975-77, 1980-83, 1989; elected to Rajya Sabha 1988, 1994. Minister of Rural Areas and Employment GOI July 1995 – May 96. President BPCC-1989-92. - E-315, Greater kailash II, New Delhi – 110 048.

Dr. KRISHAN SINGH

Son of Shivashankar Sinha.

Monghyr Zila, October 21, 1887.

M.A., B.L. (Calcutta) Ph.D.

Joined the Bar 1916; gave up Practice in response to Gandhiji's call 1920. Member and an active worker of the Indian National Congress; served Jail sentence of over eight years. Chairman Monghyr District Board, 1930. President, B.P.C.C. 1935. M.L.A., center 1935-36; First Prime Minister of Bihar, 1937-39; was member of India's constituent Assembly; Chief Minister of Bihar since 2-4-1946 to 31-1-1961.

KARPOORI THAKUR

May 1921.

Left College and Joined Quit India Movement 1942.

Leader of Opposition in Assembly. Left college and joined Quit India movement 1942. Jailed for 26 months was member of congress Socialist Party; became member of Socialist Party 1948; took part in several peasant's and agitations after independence; jailed five times; Joint Secretary Provincial Kissan Committee 1948-52. Bihar Socialist Party thrice. Bihar Branch of Socialist Party for 21 years. Chairman All India SSP, 1970-72; member State Assembly since 1952, Dep. Chief Minister Bihar Govt. 1967, 1970-72. Chief Minister 1977-79.

KEDAR PANDAY
Son of Pandit Ramphal.
Taulah, 14 June 1920.
M.Sc., L.L.B.

Congress (I) Member of Lok Sabha from Bettiah, Bihar, 1980. Chief Minister of Bihar, 1972-73. State Deputy Minister of Home, Irrigation & Power, 1957-62. Minister of Industry 1970-71. President Bihar PCC-I, 1977 & Member AICC for 25 years. Vice-Chairman Bihar, INTUC. Took part in freedom Movement 1942; Anti-Emergency agitation and was jailed. Member Bihar State Legislature, 1952-62 and 1967-80.
- Taulaha Village, Ramnagar District, West Champaran, Bihar.

KRISHNA BALLABH SAHAY
December 31, 1898.
B.A. (Hons.)

Awarded gold medal for being 1st in English Honours. Joined N.C. Movement 1920, courted jail for his political activities, 1930, 32, 33, 40 and 42; Parliamentary Secretary Bihar Cabinet; 1937. Minister for Land Revenue, Bihar, 1946-57; Piloted the Bihar Zamindari Abolition Bill 1948. Minister for co-operation & Planning, Bihar 1962-63, elected leader, Bihar Legislative Congress Party, September, 24 1963. Chief Minister Bihar since October 2, 1963 to 1967.

LALOO PRASADYADAV

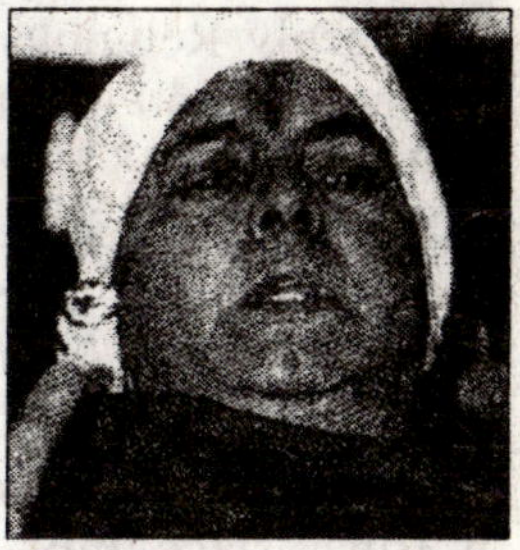

Son of Sri Kundan Rai tilled the land of Rich Land Lords. Phulwaria in Goplaganj District, Near Chapra. Now known as Saran Ammissionery, in North Bihar, 1948.

B.A., LL.B.

A Charismatic Leader. He was twice Chief Minister for Bihar since March 1990-1997. In July, 1997 after he was taken into custody and chargesheeted by the CBI for involvement in what is known as the fodder Scem involving about a Thousand Crore of rupee. Several other scandals have surfaced in Bihar involving Politicians and bureaurats.

He was President of the Janata Dal in 1996-97 but in June, 1997 he broke it up and formed the Rashtriya Janta Dal which is quite force in Bihar. At present he is Cabinet Minister of Railways in UPA Government.

MAHAMAYA PRASAD SINHA

He was Chief Minister of Bihar from 5-3-1967 to 28-1-1968.

NITISH KUMAR

Son of Kaviraj Ram Lakhan Singh

Bakhtiarput, Patna District, Bihar. 01 March 1951.

B.Sc (Engg.)

Samata Party Leader Nitish Kumar Sworn in as Bihar Chief Minister. Minister of State for few days. Agriculture & Co-operation – 21 April – 1990 10 November 1990.

Agriculture – 22 November 1999 – 02 March 2000 again 27 May 2000 – 22 July 2001. He was Railway Minister in the union cabinet. He was General Secretary, Yuva Lok Dal 1980-82. Yuva Janata 1982-83, Bihar Janata Dal 1989, President Bihar Yuva Lok Dal 1987. He was Chief Minister from 24 November 2005 to till date.

- Village Hakikatpur, P.O. Bakhtiarpur, Patna District (Bihar).

RABRI DEVI

Daughter of Sheo Prasad Choudhary

June 1959.

IV Class Pass

Deeply Religious. Rabri Devi is wife of Shri Laloo Prasad Yadav, who is President of Rashtriya Janata Dal, Chief Minister of Bihar since 25 July 1997 to Feb. 1999 win bypoll in Raghopur (margin of 61,819) and entered Bihar assembly for the first time, after four years after Chief Minister. She was elected RJD Leader in Bihar sworn in as Chief Minister, succeeding Nitish Kumar of NDA. C.M. for third time in less than three years on 11 March 2000 to date 9 April 1999-March 2000. Chief Minister of Bihar since July 1997 has been interest in the social and educational upliftment of the weaker sections of the Society.
- Chief Minister's Secretariat, Patna (Bihar).

RAM SUNDAR DASS

Shri Ram Sundar Dass was Chief Minister of Bihar from 21-4-1978 to 17-2-1980.

SARDAR HARIHAR SINGH

Self – educated mostly in Jail. Joined Freedom Movement while a student, suffered imprisonment for several terms, 21, 29, 30, 31, 40, 42, elected to Assembly, 37 46, 52 resigned from congress 57.

Chief Minister of Bihar since from 26-02-1969 to 22-06-1969.

SATISH PRASAD SINGH

Shri Satish Prasad Singh was Chief Minister of Bihar for few days e.g. from 28-1-1968 to 1-2-1968.

SATYENDRA NARAYAN SINHA

Son of Anugrah Narayan Sinha
Poiawangarh (Aurangabad, Bihar) 01 February, 1919.
M.A., L.L.B.

Advocate, Member : Syndicate of Patna and Bihar Universities 1949-60. Provisional Parliament 1950-52, Lok Sabha 1952-61, 1971-79 and 1980; of Bihar Assembly 61-67. President PCC (O) 71-77; was President Bihar Janata Party (Member of its National executive and CPB); Chief Minister of Bihar, 11-01-1989 to 06-12-1989, was member of 1977 to Lisbon 78. Joined Congress 1984.
- Baring Road, Patna.

CHIEF MINISTERS OF CHATTISGARH

Sr. No.	Name	Term of Office
1.	Ajit P.K. Jogi	- 5Dec, 2003
2.	Dr. Raman Singh	5 Dec. 2003 to till date

CHATTISGARH

AJIT P.K JOGI.
Son of K.P. Jogi
Village Pendra Road, Bilaspur (MP) 29 April, 1946.
B.E. (Mech.), M.A. College of Technology, Bhopal and L.L.B. (Delhi).

First Chief Minister of Chhattisgarh (Raipur) married to Dr. (Mrs.) Renu Jogi, October 12, 1975. Resigned from I.A.S. to join the Rajya Sabha in 1986. He was General Secretary, Madhya Pradesh Congress Committee; was Member of the A.I.C.C. on the Welfare of SC/ST; elected to Rajya Sabha in June 1986.

Dr. RAMAN SINGH
Son of Sri Vighnharan K. Thakur (Advocate)
Kabir dha Kawardhapur Village, 15 October, 1952
B.Sc 1971-72
B.A.M.S. (Ayurvedic)

He was first President (Jan Sangh) Yuva Morcha 1976-77, 1983-84. Municipal Councillor Steela Ward Kawardha.

Elected to Lok Sabha from Rajnandgaon. Later he became Union Minister of State for Commerce and Industry. Dr. Singh had quit his membership of the Lok Sabha one month after becoming the Chattisgarh State's maiden Chief Minister from the B.J.P. He was an M.L.A. from Kawardha. He was President B.J.P. He was first elected Chief Minister of Chattisgarh & Second Chief Minister of state from 5th December, 2003 till date.

Member Madhya Pradesh Vidhan Sabha 4th December, 2003.

Member Lok Sabha, 1999- .

Travel Abroad: Nepal, Philipines & Dacca in Editor of "Vidhya Vahini".

CHIEF MINISTERS OF GOA, DAMAN, DIU

Sr. No.	Name	Term of Office
1.	Dayanand B. Bandodkar	1964-66 & 67
2	Nakul Sen	18.03.1967
3.	Shashikala Kakodkar	1973-1979
4.	Pratap Singh Raoji Rane	1980-1990
5.	Luis Proto Bargosa	1990
6.	Ravi S. Naik	1991-1993
7.	Wilfred Anthony De'Souza	July 1993, 1998-99
8.	Pratap Singh Raoji Rane	1994-1998
9.	F. Sardinha	1999-2000
10.	G. Prabhu Parrikar Manohar	2000-2004
11.	Pratap Singh Raoji Rane	2004 – 16.02.2005
12.	President's Rule	17.02.2005 -
13.	Pratap Singh Rane	07.06.2005 -
14.	Digamber Kamat (19th C.M.)	08.06.2007–till date

Sh. Digamber Kamat (Congress) became 19th Chief Minister of Goa, Daman and Diu on 8th June, 2007, of a five party coaliation government. He joined Congress in 2005 only and was also Power Minister in the previous ministry.

GOA, DAMAN, DIU

DAYANAND B. BANDODKAR

12 March 1912. At Pernem knows. Postuguese, Marathi, Hindi, French and English.

A staunch nationalist, participated in the Quit India Movement, 1942, was arrested by the Portuguese for his nationalistic activities, May 13, 1956 and imprisoned for three months. He was Chief Minister of Goa, Daman & Diu. 1964 to 1966 and again from 1967 to 1973. Died on 12-08-1973.

F. SARDINHA

Goa Chief Minister F. Sardinha was Chief Minister of Goa, Daman, Diu from 1999 – and quits 24 October, 2000.

G. PRABHU PARRIKAR MANOHAR

IIT Mumbai (Metallurgical Engineering, 1978).

G. Prabhu Parrikar (BJP) is to be the new Chief Minister of Goa on 24 October 2000. In his student days on the IIT campus. "I was elected mess Co-ordinator three years in a row"; he boasts.

LUIS PROTO BARBOSA

Cansaulion, 11 January 1927.

Licin National Goa Medical College, Goa and obtain medico Circurgiao.

Married Alico Sofia Vaz. Member of Assembly since 1963 (except 1977-84); joined congress 1978, Minister of Urban Development 1985. Chief Minister of Goa 1990; was Vice President GPCC; Member Committee of Petition 1966-67, committee on Delegated Legislation 1965-66, 1967-68; served on the Panel of Presiding officers 1967-74.

- Baga, Cansaulim, Mormugao, Goa.

NAKUL SEN

14 August, 1910

Joined I.C.S. 1935, Secretary Ministery of Rehallitation 1951, Chief Secretary Punjab 1956, Secretary, Social Welfare 1966 – 67. Lt. Governor of Goa, Daman & Diu since April 18, 1967.

PRATAP SINGH RAOJI RANE
Son of Raoji Satroji Rane and Manorama Bai.
Sanquelim (Goa), 28 January 1939, married Vijaya Devi.
B.Sc. BBA

Began Political career in 1972. Member of Legislative Assembly since 1972, Cabinet Minister for Law & Judiciary, 1972-77. Chief Minister 1980-90, 1994-98. Rane is the 15th Chief Minister of Goa in the last 15 years and also Chief Minister for the seventh time.
- Golden Acres, Sanquelim (Goa).

RAVI S. NAIK
18 September 1946, married Pushpa.

An active Social Worker, Started his Political career in 1975 and joined the MGP Party (Youth Wing) became acting President. M.G.P. in 1980, was councilor, Ponda Municipal Council, 76, elected to State assembly 1984, 1989; included in ministry as Agricultural minister. All Goa Mundkar Tenant Association in October 1978 and was elected its President. He was Chief Minister of Goa 1991- May 93; Chairman Goa Kho Kho Association, also National Player of Volleyball.
- "Raikiran" Khadpabandh, Ponda, Goa.

SHASHIKALA KAKODKAR
Daughter of Dayanand Bandodkar
Pedne Village (Goa), 09 January 1935.
M.A.

Took part in Goa freedom movement; member of Assembly, 1967. Minister of State, 1973; Chief Minister of Goa 1973-79; President, Primary School Teachers Association of Goa.

WILFRED ANTHO NY DE'SOUZA
Son of Tito Fermino & Alina Anamaria
Anjuma (Bardez) 23 April 1927.
MBBS, Fellow Royal College of Surgeons of England.

President Goa PCC, 1977-80, Leader of opposition 1990-91. Minister for Public Health, PWD etc. Chief Minister of Goa since July 1993, 1998-99. President Bardez Bharat Scouts and Guides Association 1969; Member Association of Surgeons of India.

1981-83 Science & Technology and Planning. Deputy Chief Minister 1991 – May 1993.

CHIEF MINISTERS OF GUJARAT

S.No.	Name	Term of Office
1.	Ucchrangrai Naval Shanker Dhebar	1948-54
2.	Rasik Lal Umedchand Parikh	1954-56
3.	Dr. Jivraj Narayan Mehta	1960-63
4.	Balvant Rai Gopalji Mehta	1963
5.	Hitendra Kanaiya Lal Desai	1965-71
6.	President's Rule	May 1971
7.	Ghanshyam Bhai Oza	1972-73
8.	Chiman Bhai Patel	1973-74
9.	President's Rule	Feb. 1974
10.	Babu Bhai Jash Bhai Patel	1975-76
11.	Babu Bhai Jash Bhai Patel	1976
12.	President's Rule	March 1976
13.	Madhav Singh Solanki	December 1976
14.	Babu Bhai Patel	April, 1977
15.	Manek Lal Magan Lal Gandhi	1977-80
16.	President's Rule	Feb 1980
17.	Madhav Singh Solanki	1980-85
18.	Amar Singh Chaudhari	1985-89
19.	Madhav Singh Solanki	Dec. 1989
20.	Chiman Bhai Patel	March 1990
21.	Chabil Das Pragribhai Mehta	Feb. 1994
22.	Keshu Bhai Patel	March 1995
23.	Suresh Chandra Rup-Shakar Mehta	Oct. 1995
24.	President's Rule	Sep. 1996
25.	Shankar Singh Vaghela	Sep. 1996
26.	Dilip Parikha	Oct. 1997
27.	Narendra Modi	2001- till date

GUJARAT

AMAR SINGH CHAUDHRI
Son of Bhulabhai and Jatriben.
Dolvan (Dist.) Surat, 31 July 1941.
B.E. Civil.

Began career with Surat District Panchayat & worked as Hony. Architect & Engineer. First elected to the Gujarat Legislative Assembly from Vyara, constituency, 1975. was Deputy Minister for PWD in Oza Ministry, Minister for Social Welfare, December 1976; for Forest, Irrigation & Tribal Welfare 1980-85; for Home and Education March-June 1985. Founder Tribal Students Association which later merged with Gujarat Adivasi Student Association was President Vyara Taluka Youth Congress, Founder and Managing Trustee, Tribal Block Education Trust.

Chief Minister of Gujarat July 1985-November 89. President Gujarat Units of Friends of USSR & Scouts & Guides; Vice-President All India Tribal Council.

Sarita Nagar, Dulia Road, Vyara (Distt. Surat).

BABUBHAI JASHBHAI PATEL
Son of Jashbhai & Chanchal Ba.
Nadiad, (Gujarat) 09 February 1911.
B.A., L.L.B.

Former Chief Minister of Gujarat 1975-76 and 1977-1980. Member Bombay Legislative Assembly 1937 & 1946. Deputy Minister, PWD and Transport, 1952-1956. Cabinet Minister, Planning & Development 1956-57; Gujarat's Minister of PWD, Civil Supplies & Power, 1967-71 & of Finance, 1971. President Gujarat PCC, 1972-75. Vice-Chancellor, Sardar Patil University, 1958-61. Chairman Balkanji Bari Nadiad, Lok Swaraj Manch, Ahmedabad, Seva Sadan Trust Ahmedabad. Member Governing Body, Gandhi Peace Foundation, Delhi.
- "Bali", Sector-19, Plot No.26, Gandhi Nagar – 382 019 (Gujarat).

BALVANTRAY GOPALJI MEHTA
February 19, 1899.
B.A. (Bombay).

Entered Public Life, October 1920 took active part in states Peoples Movement for Civil liberties and responsible Govt. women's education, Harijan Uplift Work; started Thakkar, Bapa Harijan Ashram 1927. Member Working Committee A.I.C.C., Ex-Deputy Chief Minister Saurashtra State. Chief Minister, Gujarat State since September 19, 1963. General Secretary All India State Peoples Conference 1928-47, its Vice-President 1947-48.

CHHABILDAS PRAGIBHAI MEHTA
Son of Pragibhai Tarachand.
Mahuva (Bhavnagar District). Gujarat
Left High School to Participate in Freedom Struggle.

Member Legislative Council, 1958. Gujarat Assembly 1962-80 and since 1990 Minister for PWD, Irrigation, Roads, Building & 1973-74, Chief Whip, Congress party, 1975; Secretary Gujarat Janata Party 1984-86; General Secretary Janata Dal 1988, Chief Minister 1994. General Secretary Janata Dal 1988.
- Jalaram, Sarvoday Society, Mahuva, Distt. Bhavnagar.

CHIMANBHAI PATEL
Son of Jivabhai & Rauaben.
Chikhodra (Baroda Dist., Gujarat) 03 June 1929.
M.A.

Prof. of Economics Gujarat Vidyapith, Ahmedabad, 1953-54, joined LD Arts College 1954. Prof. Eco. & Dean of Faculty of Arts 1955-59. Principal, Sardar Vallabhbhai Parel Arts & Commerce College Ahmedabad 1960-66. Member Gujarat Assembly 1967-74; Minister of Sports, Transport & Cultural Affairs, Industries & Power 1972-73; Chief Minister 1973-74 and March 1990.
- 89, Shardanagar Society, Ahmedabad – 380 007.

Dr. JIVRAJ NARAYAN MEHTA
29 August, 1887.
L.M. & S (Bombay) M.D. (London) M.R.C.P., F.C.P.S.

He was Vice-Chairman, Gandhi Memorial Leprosy Foundation since 1952. Member Syndicate, Baroda University

1949-60, P.W.D. Minister, Bombay 1949-52. Minister for Finance Govt. of Bombay 1952-60. Chief Minister Gujarat 1960-63. Indian High Commissioner to U.K. 1963-66.

GHANSHYAMBHAI OZA
Son of Chhotalal Pitamber and Savitabahen.
Umarala (Bhavnagar Dist. Gujarat) 25 October 1911.
B.A., L.L.B.

Advocate and Social worker; member Saurashtra Assembly 1948-56, Lok Sabha 1957-67, 1971-72, Rajya Sabha since 1978. Minister for Land, Revenue, Labour Local self-Govt. 1951-56. Chairman Gujarat Industrial Development GoI. 1971-72. Chief Minister of Gujarat 1972-73.
- 2-Chandra Darshan Flats, Navrangpura, Ahmedabad (Gujarat).

HITENDRA KANAIYALAL DESAI
Son of Kanaiyalal Desai and Malvikaben.
Surat (Gujarat) 09 August 1915-12 September, 1993.
B.A., L.L.B.

Indian Politician. He was Freedom fighter, social worker and Politician. Chief Minister of Gujarat 1965-71 Cabinet Minister for works and housing – 23 December 1976-24 March 1977.

Commerce and Civil Supplies – 30 July 1979 – 13 January 1980. Appointed leader of the House since February 17, 1964 and Chief Minister from October 1, 1965-1972.

President Gujarat PCC, 1975-76, member Congress Working Committee, AICC and Parliamentary Board, 78. He was minister works and Housing 1976-77 of Commerce and Civil Supplies 1979-80.
- Sahibag, Dafnala, Ahmedabad.

KESHUBHAI PATEL
Rajkot (Gujarat) 24 July 1930.

He was Chief Minister of Gujarat State twice – in March 1995 and again in 4 March 1998 from BJP Party. Member, Gujarat Legislative Assembly 1975-80, 1980-85, 1985-90, 1990-95, 1995-97; elected to Lok Sabha 1977; Minister Irrigation and Agriculture, Govt. of Gujarat 1975-76, Public Works, 1977-80; Narmada and Water Resources, Transport and Ports. 4 March 1990-26 October 1990 Leader of Opposition Gujarat Assembly. National Vice-President Bharatiya Janata Party; since October

1995; Director Nagarik Sahakari Bank 1969-74. National Vice President Bhartiya Janata Party, since October 1995.

MADHAV SINGH SOLANKI
Son of Shri Fulsinghji
Village, Piludra, Taluka Jambusar, District Bharuch, Gujarat, 29 July, 1927.
B.A. (Hons.) L.L.B.

President, Gujarat Pradesh Congress Committee (Three times); Member (i) Legislative Assembly, Bombay, 1957-60 (ii) Legislative Assembly Gujarat, 1960-68 and Working Committee of the All India Congress Committee; was chief Minister of Gujarat in 1976, 1980-85 and again in 1990 for few months with various Portfolios of Revenue, Home, Industry, Finance, Planning etc.

Cabinet Minister for Planning & Programme Implementation 25 June 1988 – 02 December 1989.

External Affairs – 21 June 1991 – 31 March 1992 has written two books.

- Plot No. 32, Sector 19, Gandhi Nagar (Gujarat). A-4, Archita Flats, Navrangpura, Ahmedabad – 9.

MANEKLAL MAGANLAL GANDHI
Son of Maganlal Narottamdas & Mahalaxmiben.
Kalol (Panchamahals Distt. Gujarat) 27 July 1900.
Gave up studies to join freedom movement.

Was imprisoned for six and half years (1930, 1932, 1940, 1942). President Panchamals Distt. Co-operative Bank Federation. Chairman, Kalol Urban Co-operative Bank; was member of Parliament for ten years. Minister for Panchayat & Community Development, Gujarat Govt.

Member, A.I.C.C., and working committee of the G.P.C.C., Elected to the Bombay Legislative Assembly in 1937 and 1946/ Member First Lok Sabha 1952-57. Chief Minister of Gujarat 1977–1980.

- Gandhi Falia, Kalol, Gujarat.

NARENDRA DAMODARDA MODI
Vidnagar towns in Mahasana, (North-Gujarat). 17-9-1950.
M.A. (Political Science).

He became the Chief Minister of Gujarat on October 7, 2001 has developed his identity in the political arena and in the field of national awareness as an able organizer.

He dedicated himself for social services and the cause of the nation at a very young age. This patriotic fervour and nationalist spirit made him leave Vadnagar, his home town.

He came to Ahmedabad and joined the Rashtriya Swayam Sevak Sangh (RSS) and also pursued higher studies and obtained a Master Degree in Political Science.

Then Started 'Navnirman' movement in 1974 and he got the opportunity to demonstrate his leadership qualities and carve out a niche in active political work.

Recognising his potential, the party leadership made him the General Secretary of the State unit in 1988-89. He actively participated in the Somnath to Ayodha Rathyatra led by national party leader Shri L.K. Advani and subsequently the Kanyakumari to Kashmir Ekta Yatra led by Dr. Murli Manohar Joshi.

From 1989 to 1995, Shri Modi was in charge of the election campaign and during this period, the popularity of the Bharatiya Janta Party soared to new height culminating into the installation of the party's own Government with two-third majority in 1995 assembly election in the State.

The Victory of BJP under his leadership in the state has established him as a successful organizer and election strategist. Most of the media in the country recognized him as the "Architect of Gujarat B.J.P."

In the later half of 1995, the Party High Command asked him to shoulder greater party responsibility at the national level and was made the national secretary of the party in charge of various states. From 1998, Shri Modi has been working as the national General Secretary of the party till his appointment as the Chief Minister of Gujarat in October 2001.

During his political career spanning over three decades, Shri

Modi has emerged as a successful organizer, thought provoking orator, expert strategist and astute political thinker.

Shri Modi has experience of doing organizational work in the most sensitive states like Jammu and Kashmir and Punjab.

During the emergency in 1977, Shri Modi mobilized people in defiance of emergency and the arrest of national leaders.

Shri Modi has contributed many articles in newspapers and magazines. He has also authored "Sangharshman Gujarat", "Setubandhu" and Patrarup Guruji".

Widely traveled in India and abroad, Shri Modi has established close contacts with prominent political leaders.

A popular magazine published from India has ranked "Shri Modi as one of the top most leaders in the political horizon of the 21st century".

Shri Modi has carved a niche as a distinguish debater and communicator in intellectual discussion in electronic media.

Because of his rare organizational capacities, Shri Modi has acquired a permanent place in the national politics.

His return to Gujarat has electrified the spirit of BJP youth and the State party leaders are confident that the morale boosting effect of his charismatic leadership will benefit the party and the State Government.

Belongs to Mehsana district, was in ABVP before joining RSS in 1972, was loaned to BJP in 1988. Gained prominence when he joined Murli Manohar Joshi's 'EKTA YATRA' was shifted to the center after vaghela's rebellion.

Returned to Gujarat as Chief Minister in September, 2001. Known for his love of expensive clothes and designers accessories. There are also reports of his marriage to a school teacher.

An RSS pracharak, Modi came to BJP in 1988, brought in for Gujarat, ironically, by Vaghela. In 1996 he became the Party's national Secretary in charge of north India.

In 1999 he became National General Secretary, in-charge of Gujarat. Keshubhai Patel's governance had brough the party down in the dumps.

His 126-seat tally surpases previous BJP totals of 122 in 1995 and 117 in 1998. the results suggest that the BJP has gained significantly in central Gujarat – the area most affected by the riots.

RASIKLAL UMEDCHAND PARIKH

May 29, 1910.

B.Com. (London), B.Com. (Bombay)

Courted imprisonment thrice during satyagraha movement in 1930, 1933 and 1942; Member constituent Assembly 1949, elected Member Lok Sabha February 1952. Chief Minister Saurashtra, December 20, 1954 – October 31, 1956. Ex-minister for Home, Industries, Information, Electricity, Ports & Fisheries, Gujarat, 1962-63.

SHANKER SINGH VAGHELA

(Indian National Congress – Kapadvan) (Gujarat).

Shri Laxman Sinh and Smt. Nathuba.

Vasan, Distt. Gandhi Nagar. 21 July, 1940

M.A. (Economics) (Gujarat Univ).

1971-77 Organising and General Secretary, Bharatiya Jana Sangh, Gujarat.

1977 Elected to 6th Lok Sabha.

1977-78 Member, Committee on Estimates. Member Committee on Papers Laid on the Table.

1977-79 Member, Consultative Committee, Ministry of Irrigation & Agriculture.

1977-80 Vice-President, Janata Party, Gujarat.

1980-91 General Secretary and President, Bharatiya Janata Party (B.J.P.), Gujarat.

1984-89 Member, Rajya Sabha.

1984-86 Member, House Committee, Rajya Sabha

1984-89 Member, Consulative Committee, Ministry of Chemicals and Fertilizers & Ministry of Industry.

1986-87 Member, Committee on Public Undertakings.

1989 Re-elected to 9th Lok Sabha (2nd term)

1991 Member, Consultative Committee, Ministry of Petroleum and Petro-Chemicals.

1991 Re-elected to 10th Lok Sabha (3rd term1996-97 Member, Gujarat Legislative Assembly Chief Minister, Gujarat.

1999 Re-elected to 13th Lok Sabha (4th term)

1999-2000 Member, Committee on Petroleum & Chemicals.

Member, Committee on Private Members' Bills and Resolutions.

1999-2000 & 2000-2001 Member, Committee on Estimates.

Sports and Clubs : President, North Avenue MPs Club, New

Delhi (for six years).

A Former Chief Minister Vaghela Left BJP after becoming a victim of Political intrigue that involve top leaders like Atal Bihar Vajpayee, Lal Krishan Advani and Kshubhai Patel. He now has a chance to establish himself as Gujarat's tallest leader. Vaghela's strongest points are his organizing capacity, Administrative skills and political astuteness. Now he is in Congress (I) He was Chief Minister in 1996 October as B.J.P. Candidate.

- K-1, V.V.I.P. Bungalow, Sector 19, Gandhinagar – 382 019 (Gujarat). Tels. (02712) 22488m 44288. Fax. (02712) 22488
- 7, K. Kamraj Lane, New Delhi – 110 011.
Tel. (011) 23793018

SURESHCHANDRA RUP-SHANKAR MEHTA
Son of Rupshankar Mehta
Mandvi (Kutch) 16 August 1936.
B.A., L.L.B.

Worked as Civil Judge and First class Magistrate 1968-69; Member Gujarat Assembly 1975-80 and Minister of Industry, printings & Mines, Gujarat Government since 1990 and National Executive of BJP. Leader of BJP in Assembly 1985-90; Chief Minister of Gujarat Since October 1995.

- Madhavnagar, Babavadi, mandvikutch – 370465.

UCHHRANGRAI NAVAL-SHANKER DHEBAR
September 21, 1905.
B.A. L.L.B.

Chairman Khadi & Village Industries Commission since 1963. Ex-President Indian National Congress. Practised as a Lawyer in Rajkot 1929-36. Secretary Gujarat P.C.C. 1945-47, imprisoned several times in the freedom movement. Chief Minister Saurashtra 1948-54. M.P. 1962-63.

CHIEF MINISTERS OF HARYANA FROM 1-1-1966 TO DATE

S. No.	Name	Term of Office	
1.	Bhagwat Dayal Sharma	1-12-1966	23-3-1967
2.	Rao Birender Singh	24-3-1967	20-11-1967
3.	President's Rule	21-11-1967	21-5-1968
4.	Bansi Lal	21-5-1968	14-3-1972
5.	Bansi Lal	14-3-72	30-11-75
6.	Banarsi Dass Gupta	1-12-1975	29-4-1977
7.	President's Rule	30-4-1977	21-6-1977
8.	Devi Lal	21-6-1977	28-6-1979
9.	Bhajan Lal	28-6-1979	23-5-1982
10.	Bhajan Lal	23-5-1982	5-6-1986
11.	Bansi Lal	5-6-1986	20-6-1987
12.	Devi Lal	20-6-1987	2-12-1989
13.	Om Parkash Chautala	2-12-1989	23-5-1990
14.	Banarsi Dass Gupta	23-5-1990	12-7-1990
15.	Om Parkash Chautala	12-7-1990	17-7-1990
16.	Hukam Singh	17-7-1990	22-3-1991
17.	Om Parkash Chautala	22-3-1991	6-4-1991
18.	President's Rule	6-4-1991	23-6-1991
19.	Bhajan Lal	23-6-1991	10-5-1996
20.	Bansi Lal	11-5-1996	24-7-1999
21.	Om Parkash Chautala	24-7-1999	14-12-1999
22.	President's Rule	15-12-1999	01-03-2000
23.	Om Prakash Chautala	02-03-2000	-03-2005
24.	Bhupinder Singh Hooda	04-03-2005	Till date

HARYANA

BANARSI DASS GUPTA
Son of Ram Swaroop Dass.
Manheru (Bhiwani Distt) Haryana, 05 November, 1917.
Intermediate, Hindi Prabhakar.

He was President Jind State Praja Mandal General Secretary, Haryana PCC 1968-72; member Haryana Assembly, 1967-77; Speaker 1972-73; Min. for Irrigation & Power, Co-operation, Housing and Local Self Government & Agriculture, 1973-75. Chief Minister of Haryana 1975-77 AND 1987-89. Deputy Chief Minister 1989-90.

- Vijay Niwas, Vijay Nagar, Bhiwani.
- Kothi No. 1, Sector-3, Chandigarh, India.

BANSI LAL
Son of Chaudhary Mohan Singh
Golagarh, 10 October 1927, Bhiwani District (Haryana).
B.A., L.L.B.

He was Chief Minister of Haryana since 1996 – Chief Minister of Haryana 1968-75 & June 1986 to June 87.

Chief Minister of Haryana 1975-77, Member Haryana Legislative Assembly 1967, 1968-72 & 1972-75; Rajya Sabha 1960-66 and 1976-80. Punjab Pradesh Congress Committee 1958-62. Congress Working Committee 1976-77.

Defence Minister 21 December 1975-24 March 1977.

Member of Lok Sabha 1980-86 re-elected 1989; Chief Minister since June 1996-99. Railway Minister GoI, since 1985. Arrested on Charges of corruption, expelled from Indian National Congress April 1977, conduct During Emergency subject to commission of enquiry July 1977.

Awards: (1) LLD (Honours Course), by Kurukshetra University 1972. (2) Hon. D.Sc. by Haryana Agricultural University 1972.

- B.N. Chakaraborty Road, Bhiwani (Haryana).

BHAGWAT DAYAL SHARMA
Son of Murari Lal and Gulabdevi.
Berr (Rohtak Distt. Haryana) 26 January 1918.
M.A.

Participated in the Freedom Movement 1941-46, Formerly associated with INTUC; President of Punjab, Himachal Pradesh, Jammu & Kashmir, INTUC 1959-62; Member of INTUC Working Committee 1969, organizing Secretary 1971. Punjab Assembly 1962-66; Minister of State for Labour & Co-operation, Punjab Government. Member Haryana Assembly 1966-67; Chief Minister of Haryana 1966-67; Member of Rajya Sabha 1968-74 Lok Sabha.

- 17-C, North West Avenue Road, Punjabi Bagh, New Delhi–10 026.

BHAJAN LAL

Son of Kheraj and Kundana Devi

Koranwali Village, Bhawalpur State (Pakistan)

06 October, 1930.

Intermediate.

He was Chief Minister of Haryana 1978-87, 1991-95. Minister of Labour & Co-operation 1978-79; Agriculture 1970-75. Elected to Haryana Assembly four time 1968, 1972, 1977 and 1982 from Adampur. Cabinet Minister for Environment and Forests – 22 October 1986-14 February 1988.

Agriculture – 14 February 1988 – 02 December 1989. Member of Indian Delegation to World Ford Congress at Hague, 1969, U.N. 1972-73.

- Adampur Mandi, Hissar District (Haryana).

BHUPINDER SINGH HOODA

Son of Ch. Ranbir Singh, who was a member of the Committee appointed to draft the constitution of the country.

Village Sanghi in District Rohtak.

B.A., LL.B.

He was elected to Lok Sabha in 1991, 1996, 1998 and 2004. Elected to the State Assembly in the General Elections in the Year 2000 & 2005 from Kiloi Assembly constituency as a candidate of the Indian National Congress.

He was elected as the leader of the Haryana Legislature Party on March 4, 2005.

An agriculturist and advocate by Profession, President Block Congress Committee, Kiloi from 1972–77, Senior Vice-President, Haryana Pradesh Youth Congress from 1980-82, President, Haryana Pradesh Youth Congress from 1982-83, President Haryana Pardesh

Congress Committee since 1997 and Chairman Panchaya, Samiti Rohtak from 1983-87. He also served as chairman, Panchayat Parishad, Haryana from 1984-87. He was convener Haryana Congress Parliamentary Group in Parliament from 1994 to 1996 and Mmber Executive, Congress Parliamentary Party from 1994 to 1996 and Member Executive, Congress Parliamentary Party from 1994 to 1999. He is member of AICC since 1992. Served as Director, New Bank of India, 1989-92.

He has attended World Youth Festival in Mascow in 1986. World Parliamentary Conference in China, International Conference in USSR as a delegate of AICC and OISCA International Conference in Japan and South Korea.

Secretary, Jat Education, Society, Rohtak, Haryana. Member, Managing Committee, D.A.V. Educational Institution, Hassangarh, Haryana. At present Chief Minister of Haryana from March 2005 till date.

DEVI LAL

Son of Lekh Ram and Sugani.

Teja Khera, Sirsa District (Haryana)

25 September 1914-06 April, 2001.

High School.

Left Studies at the call of Mahatma Gandhi in 1930. Participated in Civil Disobedience movement, Kisan Movement & independence movement; elected to Punjab Assembly 1952-57, 1958-62, 1962-67. Member Haryana Assembly 1974-77, 1977-80; Chief Minister Haryana 1977-79, 1987-89; Leader of the Opposition, 1979-80, elected to Lok Sabha 1980-82 re-elected 1989.

Deputy Prime Minister – 02 December 1989-01 August 1990 and Minister for Agriculture – 06 December 1989 – 01 August 1990.

Deputy Prime Minister 01 November 1990 – 21 June 1991.

President PCC 1956, resigned from congress, rejoined congress 1967, became President of 1970 was detained during Emergency. Leader of the opposition 1979-80.

- Village & P.O. Chautala, Sirsa Dist. (Haryana).

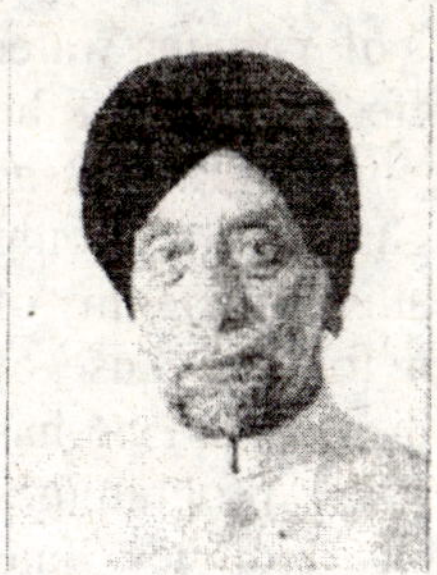

HUKUM SINGH
Charkhi Dadri (Bhiwani) 28 February 1926.
Matric.

Agriculturist; Active Trade Unionist, President Cement Employees Union of Dadri 1968-70, Peasant Labourer and Tubewell Workers Union of Dadri 1970-76; elected MLA from Dadri 1977, 82, 87; Minister for Development and Panchayats 1987-90; Chief Minister of Haryana 1990 – 22-3-1991.

OM PRAKASH CHAUTALA
Son of Ch. Devi Lal.
Chautala, Tehsil Dabwali District Sirsa (Haryana)
01 January 1935.
Studied at his native village.

Mr. Om Prakash Chautala, a great visionary assumed the office of chief Minister of Haryana for the fifth time on March 2, 2000. He had his education at his native village and later on at Sangria and Dabwali.

Being inclined towards the ideology of his father, Ch. Devi Lal, he developed from an early age a passion for politics and a strong urge to ameliorate the lot of the poor and the downtrodden.

He was also inspired by great leaders like Mahatma Gandhi and other nationalists. He has been striving hard to realize the dream of these great leaders and Ch. Devi Lal, the tallest farmer leader of our times.

Bachao', 'Samast Haryana' and 'Kisan Rally' in different parts of the State and country to create mass awakening among the people against the misrule, lawlessness and corruption prevalent at high places in the country. He stressed the need from emotional integration to strengthen the fibre of communal harmony.

Mr. Chautala was elected to the State assembly five times, 1970, 1990, 1993, 1996 and 2000. He has always been on the fore-front to safeguard the interests of Haryana. He resigned from Haryana Legislative Assembly on November 1, 1995, in protest against the then State Government's failure to safeguard the interests of people of Haryana on the issues of Yamuna water and pumping of flood water out of the flood affected areas of the State. He strongly defended Haryana's case in the Ravi-Beas waters and territorial disputes. He also highlighted the on-going poverty alleviation schemes to improve the shattered economy of the country. Being a dedicated social worker for the cause of farming community and weaker sections of the society, he has been taking keen interest in the developmental programmes being implemented for their welfare. His policies and programmes aim at strengthening India as a strong Sovereign, Socialist and Secular Democratic Republic.

Earlier, Mr. Chautala has served the State four times as Chief Minister. It was on December 2, 1989 that he first assumed the office of Chief Minister. It was again on July 12, 1990, March 22, 1991 and July 24, 1999 that he assumed the office of Chief Minister. As a result of the effective implementation of public welfare schemes during his last tenure of seven months, he was again returned from both Narwana and Rori assembly constituencies with a massive mandate. However, he opted to retain Narwana and quit Rori.

He also remained a Member of Rajya Sabha from 1987 to 1990. He became Leader of Opposition on May 24, 1996 in the ninth Haryana Vidhan Sabha. He was elected unanimously as the President of the Haryana unit of Indian National Lok Dal in 1999. He remained President of Haryana State Janata Dal and National General Secretary of the Samajwadi Janata Party. He also served as Secreatary General of the Samajwadi Janata Party and Chief of the Kisan Kamgar Cell of All India Lok Dal.

Mr. Chautala was also appointed Convener of Anti-Dunkel Rally held on March 18, 1994 at Delhi. He also remained member of important committees of the Lok Sabha, Rajya Sabha and Haryana Vidhan Sabha. At present, he is president of the Indian National Lok Dal.

Mr. Chautala has not only organized a number of conferences and rallies, but also attended several national and international conferences. He has toured extensively in the country and abroad. The countries visited by him include United States of America, UK, Germany, France, Spain, Portugal, Australia, Japan, Holland, Pakistan, Canada, Newzealand, Singapore, Greece etc.

RAO BIRENDRA SINGH
Son of Balbir Singh & Nihal Kaur
Rewari (Haryana) 20 February 1921.
B.A.

Served in the Army as Commissioned Officer 1942-47. Politician. Member Lok Sabha, since 1980 was minister Govt. of Punjab, 1956-61. Chief Minister of Haryana, 1961. Leader of the opposition Haryana Vidhan Sabha 1968-71. Union Minister for Agriculture & Rural Development, 1980-84; Food & Civil supplies January – September 1985. Member Congress Party 1954-67. Founder Vishal Haryana Party 1967. Rejoined Congress (I) after merging his party with it in 1978. Chief Minister of SVD Govt., March – November 1967. Member Lok Sabha 1971-77.

- Village Rampura, P.O. Rewari, Distt. Mohindergo, Haryana.

CHIEF MINISTERS OF HIMACHAL PRADESH

S. No.	Name	Term of Office
1.	Dr. Y. S. Parmar	1952 – 1957 – 1962
2.	Dr. Y. S. Parmar	1962 – 67
3.	Dr. Y. S. Parmar	1967 – 72
4.	Dr. Y. S. Parmar	1972 – 77
5.	Ram Lal	Jan 1977 – March 1977
6.	Shanta Kumar	June 1977 – 1980
7.	Ram Lal	1980 – 82
8.	Ram Lal	1982 – 83
9.	Vir Bhadra Singh	1983 – 85
10.	Vir Bhadra Singh	1985 – 90
11.	Shanta Kumar	1990 – 92
12.	Vir Bhadra Singh	1996 – 98
13.	Vir Bhadra Singh	March 1998 – 12 Days
14.	Prem Kumar Dhumal	1998 – 2003 Feb.
15.	Vir Bhadra Singh	March 2003 – till date

HIMACHAL PRADESH

PREM KUMAR DHUMAL
Son of Capt. Mahant Ram
Samirpur Dist. Hamirpur (HP) 10 April 1944.
M.A. (English), Degree in Law.

He was Chief Minister of Himachal Pradesh since March 1998 – February 2003. General Secretary College Students Central Association 1967-68. General Secretary, College Teachers Union, 1973-77. President College Teachers Union 1977-80. Secretary State BJP 1985-87. Gen.Secretary H.P. B.J.P. 1987-93. President H.P. BJP 1993-98 Member 9th Lok Sabha.
- H.P. Secretariat, Simla (HP).

RAMLAL
Son of Nazarlal
Bharthata (Haryana).
B.A., L.L.B.

Former Chief Minister of Himachal Pradesh, 1980-83, elected Member, HP Assembly 1962 was Chief Whip of HP congress Legislative Party & also Chief Parliamentary Secretary in 1966. Minister for Education, civil supplies & co-operation until 1972; Minister PWD 1972-77. Sworn in as Chief Minister Jan. 1977 – March 77, 1980 – 82, 1982 – 83.
- At & Post Village, Bharthala, Haryana.

SHANTA KUMAR
[Bharatiya Janata Party – Kangra (Himachal Pradesh)].
Jagannath Sharma and Smt. Kaushalya Devi.
Garhjamula, Distt. Kangra, 12 September, 1934 (HP).
Married Smt. Santosh Shailja
B.A., L.L.B.

1965-68 President, Zila Parishad, Kangra.

1972-85 Member, Himachal Pradesh Legislative Assembly.

1977-80 Chief Minister, Himachal Pradesh.

1980-85 Leader of the opposition, Himachal Pradesh, Legislative Assembly.

1989 Elected to 9th Lok Sabha

1990-92 Member, Himachal Pradesh Legislative Assembly.

Chief Minister, Himachal Pradesh (2nd term).

1998 Re-elected to 12th Lok Sabha (2nd term).

1998-99 Member, Rules Committee

Member, Committee on Defence and its Sub-Committee-I

Member, Library Committee.

Member, Consultative Committee, Ministry of Power.

1999 Re-elected to 13th Lok Sabha (3rd term).

Books Published : (i) Dharti Balidan Ki; (ii) Himalaya Par Lal Chhaya; (iii) Desh Bhakta Sanyasi; (iv) Lajo; (v) Manke Meet; (vi) Kaidi; (vii) Mrigtrishna; (viii) Rajniti Ki Shatranj; (ix) O Pravasee Meet Mere; (x) Jyotirmayi; and (xi) Jail Diary (all in Hindi), Vivekanad, Man Ki Meet, Quidi etc.

Health, meditation and yoga

Gardening, cooking and playing with children

Countries Visited : Pakistan and U.S.A. – for treatment only.

Leader of Opposition, Himachal Vidhan Sabha 1980-84. Vice President Kangra Zilla Parishad, 1964; M.L.A. 1972 & Chief Minister 1977.

Cabinet Minister for Consumer Affairs & Public Distribution 13 October 1999- Chief Minister of HP – 1977-80, elected to Lok Sabha 89. Chief Minister 1990-93 was detailed during emergency.

- Yamini Complex, Palampur, District Kangra-176 061. (Himachal Pradesh). Tels. (01894) 30630, 30632,
Fax (01894) 32588.

- 9, Janpath, New Delhi – 110 011. Tels. (011) 23388165, 23382756 (O), 23012287, 23012253 (R)

VIRBHADRA SINGH

Son of Raja Sir Padam Singh

Sarahan, Mahasu (Himachal Pradesh)

23 June 1934.

B.A. (Hons), M.A.

He is Chief Minister of Himachal Pradesh since April 1983-89 and November 1993 – March 98. Elected to Parliament in 1980. Became Deputy Minister for Tourism & Civil Aviation 31 December 1976 – 24

March 1977. Minister of State for Industry – 11 September 1982 – 08 April 1983. Member of Lok Sabha 1962 – 82 & Himachal PCC.

Former ruler of Bushahr State, now part of Himachal Pradesh.

President HPCC 1977-79, Member Estimate Committee of Lok Sabha 1980-82.

He became Chief Minister of Himachal Pradesh, since February, 2003 – till date.

Honorary Captain in the Indian Army, Member of Indian Delegation to the General Assembly of the United Nations, 1976; In 1990 he was elected to State Assembly from Rohru Constituency. He remained President of HPCC from 1992-94. In 1993 he was again elected to State Legislative Assembly and became Chief Minister 3 December, 1993 to 24 March 1998. Associated with various cultural and social organizations. Remained President, Sanskrit Sahitya Sammelan and Friends of Soviet Union Society (H.P. State Branch).

- Padma Palace, P.O. Rampur (Bushahr), Simla District (H.P.).

Dr. Y.S. PARMAR

Son of Bhandari Shivanand Singh Parmar & Lakshmi Devi.

Chanhalag, District Sirmur, August 4, 1906.

M.A., L.L.B., Ph.D.

Indian Lawyer, agriculturist and politician. Served Sirmur state, 1930-41, resigned due to political differences and exiled from the state 1941, successfully organized satyagraha in Suket State, culminating in the integration of Hill States into Himachal Pradesh, nominated to A.I.C.C., 1948; Member, Chief Commissioner's Advisory Council 1948; constituent Assembly, September 1949. President, HPCC; 1948-50. M.P., 1957; President HPCC, Chief Minister of Himachal Pradesh 1957-62, 1962 – 67, 1967 – 72, 1972 – 77.

Publication : (1) Social and Economic Background of Himalayan Polyandry. (2) Himachal Pradesh – Its proper shape and status.

Years of Challenge and growth 1975.

CHIEF MINISTERS OF JAMMU AND KASHMIR

S. No.	Name	Term of Office
1.	Sheikh Mohammad Abdullah	1948-53
2.	Ghulam Mohammad Sadiq	1964-
3.	Syed Mir Qasim	1972-75
4.	Sheikh Mohammad Abdullah	1975-77
5.	Dr. Farooq Abdullah	1982-84
6.	Ghulam Mohammad Shah	1984-86
7.	Dr. Farooq Abdullah	1986-90
8.	Dr. Farooq Abdullah	1996
9.	Mufti Muhammad Sayeed	2002 to 2006
10.	Gulam Nabi Azad	2-112005 – Till Date

GULAM NABI AZAD

He was born in March 1949 at Village Soti in Doda, J&K District. He had his M.Sc. Zoology from Kashmir University in 1972. He joined politics in 1973, from 1973 to 75 remained Block Secretary of Congrss Committee, Blessa. In 1975 Mr. Azad was nominated as President of Jammu and Kashmir Pradesh Youth Congress. In 1977 he was appointed as President of Jammu and Kashmir Pradesh Youth Congress. In 1977 he was appointed as President of Congress Committee, Doda District. During this year, he was nominated as General Secretary of All India Youth Congress. Besides this, from 1978 to 1981 he remained the President of All India Muslim Youth Conference. He was nominated as member of Congress Working Committee in 1986 and nominated as General Secretary of AICC in 1987 and elected as General Secretary for nine times.

Mr. Azad was inducted as Union Deputy Minister for Company Affairs and Law in 1982 and later took over as Minister of State in this Ministry. In 1985 he was again elected as Member Parliament from Washin Constituency and got birth in Union Cabinet as Minister of State for Home Affairs and later he was given Food and Civil Supplies portfolio. In 1990 Mr. Azad was elected as Rajya Sabha Member and in 1991 Mr. Narisimha Rao Ministry he was inducted as Cabinet Minister for Parliamentary Affairs and later given Tourism and Civil Aviation portfolio. Mr. Azad was made President of JKPCC under whose guidance Assembly elections in 2002 Congress bagged 21 seats and thus became the second largest party in the Assembly.

Mr. Azad was Union Minister for Urban Development and Law & Parliamentary Affairs in present Dr. Manmohan Singh UPA Government till he resigned to take over as Chief Minister of J&K State.

Mr. Ghulam Nabi Azad is the 3rd Congress Chief Minister after Mr. G.M. Sadiq and Syed Mir Qasim.

He was sworn in on 2nd November, 2005 to till date.

JAMMU & KASHMIR

Dr. FAROOQ ABDULLAH
Son of Sheikh Mohammad Abdullah & Akbar Jahan
Srinagar, J & K, 21 October 1937.
M.B.B.S.

He was Chief Minister of Jammu and Kashmir 1982-84. President J & K National conference; J & K Cricket Association, Chairman J & K State Centre Labour Union. Chief Minister since October 1996, during 1986 March – 90. Chairman J & K Muslim Auqub Trust; Sher-i-Kashmir, National Medical Institute Trust. Chief Minister 1986 March 90.
- 10 Maulana Azad Road, Srinagar (J & K).

GHULAM MOHAMMAD SADIQ
1912
B.A., L.L.B.

Elected member first state Legislative Assembly, 1934; courted arrest in agitation against Govt. in 1938. Chairman, National Conference 1939. Deputy Minister 1948-51, elected President, J & K Assembly 1951. Chief Minister, Jammu & Kashmir state since February 28, 1964.

GHULAM MOHAMMAD SHAH
Son of Khawaja Mohammad Shah
Srinagar, J&K 20 July 1920.
B.A., L.L.B., Fellow London School of Economics.

Chief Minister of Jammu & Kashmir July 1984 to March 1986. Son-in-law of the Late Sheikh Mohammad Abullah, Lion of Kashmir. Joined the National Conference, 1944, was detained in Jail for a year in the Quit Kashmir Movement. He was Vice-President All J & K National

Conference. Founded Holy Eelic Action Committee, Minister of State 1975, Min. of Food Supplies.
- 10 Maulana Azad Road, Srinagar (Kashmir).

MUFTI MUHAMMAD SAYEED

Brijbehara in Anantnag District on January 12, 1936.

Studied at SP College in Srinagar and went to Aligarh to pursue his Master's and Law and Post Graduation in Arabic.

Mufti was member of the State Legislative Assembly from 1962 to 1972, followed by five years as member of the Legislative Council. He was deputy minister of agriculture and cooperation and Minister of Works and Urban development.

He came close to becoming the Chief Minister in 1976 when the Congress withdraw its support to the government led by Sheikh Mohammad Abdullah, the N.C. Founder. A long time critic of the National Conference, he has a running feud with Farooq Abdullah, who blames him for the dismissal of his government in 1984 and 1990.

Mufti had crossed over to the Janata Dal in 1987 and became union home minister in the V.P. Singh government from December 1989 to November 1990. He was elected to the Rajya Sabha in 1986 and again in 1992, but resigned in 1996.

He revived the congress in the valley and won the Anantnag Lok Sabha seat. He was state President of Congress in September 1996. He coaxed his daughter Mehbooba of enter politics and fight the election from their home-town in Bijbehera. Mehbooba's mother Gulshan also joined the fray from Pahalgam. But exercise yielded little. The congress lost everywhere in the valley except at Bijbehara. His three-year old party makes a clean sweep of Valley, demolishing what has been considered the bastion of the NC.

Political analysts call it a major paradigm shift in the history of the troubled Jammu and Kashmir State. The People's Democratic Party (PDP) Government will function under the common Minimum Programme (CMP) which has been drafted after consensus of every issue. PDP has to strictly follow the

CMP, which, of course, is not pro-separatist.

Mufti Sayeed was administered oath of confidence at a simple function in the Sprawling International convention complex at the shores of Dal Lake on November 2, 2002, new Chief Minister of J & K. Congress President Sonia Gandhi, former union Minister C.K. Jaffer Sharief, Ambika soni, Manmohan Singh were present on the occasion.

The swearing in of Mufti Muhammad Sayeed as the Chief Minister of Jammu and Kashmir is a defining moment in the political history of the state. The event represents a blending of local aspirations and national objectives with an overwhelming public approval. And, the man of the moment brings with him to the high post a rich combination of a long political tapassiya, administrative acumen, clean public image and an uncompromising stand on the rights of his people.

A seasoned politician who played a significant role on the political stage of Jammu and Kashmir since he was initiated into politics in early 1950s. On his return, he practiced as a lawyer for some time but was actually attracted to politics. Since then, it is a long and impressive innings in public life that saw him holding high offices including those an ministers at the state and union levels.

Mufti Sahab was elected to the State Assembly for the first time in 1962. He was again returned to the Assembly in 1967 following which he was inducted into the State Council of Ministers as a deputy minister for Agriculture and Cooperation. But, he was soon to resign from the ministry as his first expression of dissent involving his political principles. He was appointed a cabinet minister in 1972 in the government led by Syed Mir Qasim in which he held the important portfolios of Works, Urban Development and Education. He was a member of the legislative council between 1972 and 1975.

Following the return to power of the late Sheikh Mohammad Abdullah in 1975 with congress suppot, Mufdti Mohammad Sayeed headed the state unit of Indian National Congress. He retained that post for twelve long years and became the symbol and focal point of a credible and issue based opposition in the state.

In 1986, Mufti Saheb moved to the national politics and became a member of the Rajya Sabha. Same year, Rajiv Gandhi inducted him into his cabinet as the minister of tourism. However, a year later he resigned to register his protest against the manner in which important decisions about the sensitive state were taken. Keeping with his high moral standards he resigned the Rajya Sabha seat to which he was elected on Congress ticket. He joined the Janata Dal led by VP Singh and successfully contested Lok Sabha election from Muzaffarnagar in 1989. He was appointed the Union Minister in the V.P. Singh ministry. In1998, he was elected to the Lok Sabha from Anantnag constituency as a Congress party candidate.

A year later, he launched J&K Peoples' Democratic Party, a regional political forum, which found almost an instant acceptability. Mufti Muhammad Sayeed saw the young party taking center stage in Kashmir politics and bloomin into a credible and authentic voice of its people. His agenda of peace with dignity, balanced development and sincere expression of concerns of the people received a resounding endorsement from the electorate which is now reflected in the constitution of the new state cabinet.

Mufti Muhammad Sayeed is a widely traveled person having friends, admirers and political colleagues all over the country. His statesman status is acknowledged by the entire political spectrum cutting across personal affiliations.

SHEIKH MOHAMMAD ABDULLAH
Son of Sheikh Mohammad Ibrahim.
5 December 1906 — 8 September, 1982 .
M.Sc.

Indian Political Leader and founder of National Conference. Chief Minister of Jammu & Kashmir, popularly known as Sher-a-Kashmir (born of Kashmir).

He was Chief Minister of J & K February 1975 – March 1977. Member delegation from India to U.N.O., detained 1953 – April 7, 1964, 1965-68 in exile 1971-72. Head of the Interim government Nov. 1947, Member Indian delegation to UN Jan 1948; Chief Minister of Jammu & Kashmir 1948-53. Member Indian Consitituent Assembly 1949; Leader State Congress Party 1975-77.

SYED MIR QASIM
Son of Mir Mohammad Shah
Dooru, Sahahabad, Anantnag (J & K) 16.01.1919 – 12.12.2004.
M.A., L.L.B.

He joined politics in late 1940's when he was nominated into the constituent assembly in 1950 to represent Dooru Consituency. He was elected the First President of Congress in 1965 when G.M. Sadiq merged the National Conference into Congress.

Chief Minister of Jammu & Kashmir 1972-75. Joined politics, 1943, arrested during Quit Kashmir movement, 1946. Member Constituent Assembly 1951-57. Chief Parliamentary Secretary, 1952, Minister for Revenue, 1953-57, for Irrigation power & Law, 1961-62, for Revenue & Rehabilitation, 1962-63. President J & K PCC, 1965-71.

Cabinet Minister without Port folio – 07 June – 08 August 1976.

Civil Supplies & Co-operation – 08 August 1976 – 24 March 1977.

- Doru, Shahabad, Anantnag (J & K).

CHIEF MINISTERS OF JHARKHAND

Sr. No.	Name	Term of Office
1.	Babu Lal Marandi	First Chief Minister 15.11.200.... to 16.03.2003
2.	Arjun Munda	17.03.2003 to 03.03.2005
3.	Shibu Soren	03.03.2005 to 10.03.2005
4.	Arjun Munda	18.03.2005 to 17.09.2006
5.	Madhu Koda	18.09.2006 to Till Date

MADHU KODA

Independent Legislator Madhu Koda was sworn in as Chief Minister of Jharkhand on 18 September, 2006.

Koda, who has the support of 42 legislators in a house of 82 members, has been asked by the Governor to prove his majority by September 25.

The UPA decided to set-up three committees to guide the Koda Government in Policy-formulation and decision-making. Of the three committees, the UPA Steering Committee and the co-ordination committee will be headed by JMM President Sibu Soren.The third, the advisory committee, will be headed by Political thinkers.

When Madhu Koda took over as Chief Minister of Jharkhand, he set a series of records :

(1) C M Number 5 : He is the fifth chief minister since the formation of the state in 2000. Babulal Marandi was the first, Munda was chief minister twice and Sibu Soren headed the government for nine days.

(2) Independent Head : He is the third Independent Legislator to head the State after Bishwanath Das of Orissa (1971) and F.A. Khonglam of Meghalaya (2002).

(3) Youthful Charge : At 35, he is the second youngest Chief Minister after Assam's Prafulla Kumar Mohanta.

(4) Numbers Game : JMM : 17, Congress : 9, RJD : 7, UGDP : 2, AIFB : 2, Independent : 4, NCP : 1

JHARKHAND

All important major minerals like iron, coal, aluminium, uranium etc. are found in abundance below the fertile soil of Jharkhand.

ARJUN MUNDA

The BJP Legislative Party on 17th March 2003 Unanimously elected Arjun Munda welfare Minister in the Babulal Marandi government, as its leader. BJP general secretary Rajnath Singh claimed that the NDA would stake its claim to form the Government with the support of all the seven rebel ministers, who had crossed the floor of the House demanding Marandi's removal.

Arjun Munda, former Welfare Minister and a relatively late entrant into the BJP, was Sworm in as the Chief Minister of Jharkhand on 17-3-2003 (Tuesday) Munda, a Legislator from Kharsawa in east singhhum is the second Chief Minister of Jharkand state 17.03.2003 till 03.03.2005 and 18.03.2005 to till date.

BABULAL MARANDI

Son of Chhotu Lal Marandi

Kodai Bank, Giridih District (Jharkand) 11 January 1958.

Graduate

He was Minister of State for Environment & Forests – 19 March 1998 – 07 November 2000. He was the first Chief Minister of Jharkand state 15.11.2000 to 16.03.2003.

- Power House Road, Barganda, Giridih (Jharkand).

SHIBU SOREN

Elected Chief Minister on 01.03.2005 and remained till 10.03.2005 and resigned, since could not prove majority on the floor of the house.

CHIEF MINISTERS OF KARNATAKA

S. No.	Name	Term of Office
1.	K. Chengalaraya Reddy	25-10-1947 to 30-03-1952
2.	Kengal Hanumadithaiya	30-03-1952 to 19-08-1956
3.	Kadidal Manjappa	19-08-1956 to 31-10-1956
4.	S. Nijalingappa	01-11-1956 to 19-04-1957
	S. Nijalingappa	19-04-1957 to 16-05-1958
5.	B.D. Jatti	16-05-1958 to 09-03-1962
6.	S. R. Kanthi	09-03-1962 to 20-06-1962
7.	S. Nijalingappa	21-06-1962 to 03-03-1967
	S. Nijalingappa	03-03-1967 to 29-05-1968
8.	Veerendra Patil	29-05-1968 to 27-03-1971
	President's Rule	27-03-1971 to 20-03-1972
9.	D. Devaraj Urs	23-03-1972 to 31-12-1977
	President's Rule	31-12-1977 to 28-021978
10.	D. Devaraj Urs	28-02-1978 to 07-01-1980
11.	R. Gundurao	12-01-1980 to 07-01-1983
12.	Ramakrishna Hegde	10-01-1983 to 02-01-1985
	Ramakrishna Hegde	08-03-1985 to 13-02-1986
	Ramakrishna Hegde	16-02-1986 to 11-08-1988
	Ramakrishna Hegde	13-08-1988 to 21-04-1989
13.	S. R. Bommai	13-08-1988 to 21-04-1989
	President's Rule	21-03-1989 to 30-11-1989
14.	Veerendra Patil	30-11-1989 to 10-10-1990
	President's Rule	10-10-1990 to 17-10-1990
15.	S. Bangarappa	17-10-1990 to 19-11-1992
16.	M. Veerappa Moily	19-11-1992 to 10-12-1994
17.	H. D. Devegowda	11-12-1994 to 31-05-1996
18.	J. H. Patel	31-05-1996 to 10-10-1999
19.	S. M. Krishna	11-10-1999 to 27-05-2004
20.	N. Dharam Singh	28-05-2004 to 02-02-2006
21.	H.D. Kumaraswamy	03-02-2006 to Till Date

KARNATAKA

Karnataka is the eighth largest state in India both in Area and population. It was formerly known as Mysore. On November 1, 1973 the name Mysore was changed to Karnataka.

BASAPPA DANAPPA JATTI
Son of Danappa & Bhagavva
Savalgi, (Karnataka), 10 September 1912.
B.A., L.L.B.

Minister for Finance, Govt. of Karnataka, 1962-65. Minister for Food & Civil Supplies, 1965-68. Lt. Governor of Pondicherry 1968-1972. Governor of Orissa 1972-74. President Jamkhandi Municipality 1940-45. Chief Minister Jamkhandi State 1946-48. Deputy Minister for Health & Labour 1952-56. Received Hony LLD from Karnataka University 1974; Guru Nanak Dev University 1978; Behrampur University 1977. Chief Minister of Karnataka 16-05-1958 to 09-03-1962. Vice-President of India 1974-1979. Acting President of India 11 February 1977 to 25 July, 1977.
- Shivananda, 224 Bellary Road, Bangalore.

C.M. POONCHA
Son of C.T. Muthanna
Attur Village, South Coorg. (Karnataka).
1910-03 August, 1990
St. Aloysius College, Managalore.

Elected to Constitutional Assembly and Provisional Parliament 1947-51; Sentence to imprisonment 1932, 33, detained during Quit India Movement 1942. Minister of State for Civil Aviation 1966.

Minister for Transport & Aviation 1966-1967.

Cabinet Minister for Railway 1967-1969.

Chief Minister 1952-56.

Leader Trade Delegations to various countries 1961, 1963. Member of Rajya Sabha 1964; Governor Madhya Pradesh August, 1978-_____; Chairman , mahahar Chemicals and Fertilizers Ltd. 1970-1971.

D. DEVRAJ URS
August 20, 1915-6 June, 1982
B. Sc.

He was Chief Minister of Karnataka 1972-1977 and 1978-1980. Assume office as Chief Minister on 20 May, 1972. Member Assembly 1941-48. Took part in Quiet India Movement, 1942; Participated in the struggle for Responsible Government in Mysore, 1947. Member Legislative Assembly since 1952 from Hunsun Constituency; Minister for Labour, Transport of Tourism, Karnataka State 1962-68; was Chairman Central Silk Board; Convener, K.P.C.C. Chief Minister, Karnataka State since March 20, 1972-77 & 1971-80.

H.D. DEVE GOWDA
Son of Haradanahalli (Karnataka)
18 May 1933.
Civil Engineer

Ran Contracting business, elected to Karnataka State Legislative in 1960's; Imprisoned during State of Emergency in 1970's.

The Leader of the United Front and former Karnataka Chief Minister December 1994 – May 1996 was the 11th Prime Minister of India from June 1, 1996 to April 21, 1997, waited 32 years before he got elected as Karnataka Chief Minister in November 1994. Became President of Janata Dal (Secular), following split in the Party. Lost the 1999 election to the Lok Sabha. Member Karnataka Legislative Assembly 1962-96, elected to Rajya 1996, Lok Sabha 1998; Life member Karnataka Branch of commonwealth Parliamentary Association.
- Holenarasipur, Hassan Dist. Karnataka.

J.H. PATEL
Son of Halappa Patel and Smt. Mahadevamma
1ST October, 1930
B.A. (Mysore) LL.B.

Father Halappa Patel had represented Channagiri as MRA.

This tradition has been continued by J. H. Patel.

Participated in the freedom struggle in 1947 and underwent imprisonment in the process.

From 1947 till date continues to fight against in justice and has underwent imprisonment in the process.

Considers Shri Ram Manohar Lohia as Guru and a close associate of Sriyuths. Shanthaveera Gopala Gowda, George Fernandes, Madhu Limave and others.

Served Jail term for participating directly in the Satyagraha.

Close associate of Shri U. R. Ananthamurthy, Jnana Peeta Awardee Shri Gopala Krishna Adiga Beechi and Shri P.Kalinga Rao. Has a flair for literature, satire and music.

Elected to Lok Sabha from Shimoga Constituency in 1967.

Protested against emergency and was imprisoned in Shimoga, Gulbarg and Bangalore.

Elected to the Legislative Assembly from Channagiri constituency in 1978 led struggle for the cause of the Backward classes and the downtrodden, being in the opposition.

Eleected for the second term to the Legislative Assembly from Channagiri Constituency and served as Minister in 1983.

Resigned in 1984 as Minister as a measure to strengthen the party.

Re-elected in 1985 from Channagiri constituency and served as Minister.

Instrumental in forming Janata Dal in 1989, became President of Janata Dal, strived to bring the party to power.

In the Assembly elections of November-December 1994, Janta Dal was elected as the single largest party.

Sworn in as Deputy Chief Minister of Karnataka on 11th December 1994 after winning with a huge margin in the elections.

Holds the portfolio of Power (which is the basic necessity to Agricultural and Industrial sectors) and Tourism.

Smt. Sarvamangala, wife of Sri J. H. Patel and three sons have been a constant source of inspiration to J. H. Patel.

Believes in driving away the evil practice of untouchability from the minds of people. Chief Minister of Karnataka 31-05-1996 to 10-10-1999.

KENGAL HANUMANTHAIYA
Son of Venkata Gowda
Kengeri Lakkapanahalli, Bangalore Distt. (Karnataka)
06 Feb. 1908-01 Dec, 1980.
B.A., L.L.B. Married Smt. Puttamma, May, 1934.

Advocate; President, Bangalore Municipal Council, 1942, President Bangalore D.C.C. for ten years. Member of the Executive Committee of the Constituent Assembly, and Provisional Parliament; Leader of the Congress Party in Mysore Legislative Assembly, 1952-56; Cabinet Minister for Law and Social Welfare – 26 June 1970 – 18 March 1971.

Railways 18 March 1971 – 22 July 1972.

Chief Minister of Mysore, 1952-56; nationalised Kolar Gold Mines, integrated Karnataka; M.L.A. Mysore 1952 & 1956, elected to Lok Sabha 1972 & 1967; Chairman, the Punjab Administrative Reforms Commission 1964-65; Leader, Indian Delegation to Commonwealth Parliamentary Conference Ottava, 1966. Deputy Leader Congress Party in Lok Sabha, 1967-68.

Awarded "Rashtra Rathna" title 1973.

KYSASAMBALLY CHENGALARAYA REDDY.
Son of B. Venkata Reddy.
Rajupet (A.P.) 04 May 1902-27 February, 1976.
B.A., L.L.B.

Member Mysore Legislature 1930-52; President Kolar District Board 1933-37. Member Working Committee Mysore Congress 1937-52. Leader Parliamentary Party 1937-52. President 1937-38 and 1946-47; member constituent Assembly of India 1947-50; Launched Satyagraha for the establishment of responsible government in Mysore state 1947-50. Chief Minister of Mysore state 1947-52; member Council of states 1952-57; M.P. (Loksabha) 1957. 1962-65. Governor of Madhya Pradesh 1965-77.

M. VERAPPA MOILY

Shri M. Veerappa Moily was Chief Minister of Karnataka from 19-11-1992 to 10-12-1994.

KADIDAL MANJAPPA
1910.
B.A., L.L.B.

Minister for Revenue, Mysore, since May 1958. Participated in all the freedom movements elected leader, Mysore Assembly congress Party August 16, 1956; Chief Minister August – October 1956. Minister for Education till second general elections; elected to the state Assembly, 1957.

N. DHARAM SINGH
1936

Sri N. Dharam Singh was sworn in as Chief Minister heading a Congress- JD (S) coalition on 28 May, 2004. Amiable and non-controversal, Singh belongs to the minority community of Rajputs in Karnataka. Singh has never lost an election. He has now been elected from the Jewargi Assembly constituency for Right times, starting from 1972. Singh admitted that though both the Congress and JD (S) "fought each other" in the elections, they came together as both were secular and share the concern for farmers, weaker sections, Dalits and minorities. Singh became the 17th Chief Minister of the state, the third backward classes representative to occupy the Post.

Dharam Singh is the Patron of the Mahasabha and is instrumental in setting up the Mahasabha.

OSCAR FERNANDES
Son of Roque Fernandes.
Udupi, 27 March 1941.
B.A.

Politician, Member of Parliament. First elected to Parliament (Lok Sabha) in 1980 from Udipi (Karnataka) defeating Shri T.A. Pai, a former Union Minister. Re-elected in 1984. Appointed Chief Minister of Karnataka Pradesh Congress Committee (I) in January 1986. Member of Indian delegation to UNCTAD, Bangalore.

- B-202, M.S. Flats, Baba Kharaksingh Marg,
  New Delhi – 110 001.

R. GUNDU RAO

Kushalnagar, Coorg Dist., Karnataka, 08 April 1937.

Intermediate.

Joined Congress, 1965 was member; DCC Coorg and Secretary Youth Congress Coorg; took part in All India Youth Congress Conference, convenor and President of Karnataka and became Minister of State for Information and youth services. Leader of opposition in Assembly for some time; Chief Minister 1980-83.

- Kushalnagar, Somwarpet Taluk, Coorg, Dist., (Karnataka).

RAMAKRISHNA HEGDE

Son of Mahabaleshwar Hegde and Saraswati.

Siddhapur (Karanataka) 29 August 1926.

M.A., L.L.B.

Deputy Minister for Planning & Development Karnataka Government, 1957-58. General Secretary KPCC 1958-62. Chief Minister of Karnataka.

1. 10-01-1983 to 02-01-1985
2. 08-03-0985 to 13-02-1985
3. 16-02-1986 to 11-08-1988
4. 13-08-1988 to 21-04-1989

Deputy Chairman Planning Commission, December 1989 – November 1990; President World Federation to UN Association. Cabinet Minister for Commerce – 19 March 1998 – 13 October 1999.

- "Kritika", 229 Rajmahalvilas Extn., Bangalore (Karnataka).

S. BANGARAPPA

[India National Congress – Shimoga (Karnataka)]

Shri Kallappa and Smt. Kallamma.

26 October 1933.

B.A., B.L., Diploma in Social Science Agriculturist and Lawyer.

Position Held

1967-96 Member, Karnataka Legislative Assembly

1977-78 Minister of State, Home, Karnataka

1978-79 Cabinet Minister, P.W.D., Karnataka

1979-80 President, Pradesh Congress Committee [P.C.C. (I)] Karnataka

1980-81Minister, Revenue and Agriculture, Karnataka

1985-1987 Leader of Opposition, Karnataka Legislative Assembly.

He was Chief Minister 1990-92. Member of Assembly since 1967, formerly associated with SSP joined Congress 1976. Minister of State for KPCC 1979, Leader of Opposition 1985. Chief Minister of Karnataka 1990-92; elected to Lok Sabha 1996.

- 7-B, Janpath, New Delhi – 110 001.

S. NIJALINGAPPA

Son of Adivappa & Neelamma

Haluvagulu (Beltary Distt, Karnataka) 10 December, 1902 – 08 August, 2000.

B.A. (Bangalore) L.L.B. (Poona).

Enrolled as advocate of Mysore High Court 1926. Joined congress 1924, took part in freedom struggle, debarred form Legal Practice, 1940. Jailed 1939, 1942-44, 1947; President Mysore PCC 1945-46, of Karnataka PCC 1945-54 of Mysore PCC 1960-62. Member, Constituent Assembly 1946-50. Parliament 1950-56. Chairman Indian Oil Co. Ltd. until 1962. Chief Minister (1) 1956-1958 & (2) 1962-68. President Indian National Congress (O) 1968-71. Chairman Sardar Patel Memorial Trust, Sucheta Kripalani Memorial Trust, L.B. Shastri National Memorial Trust; Awarded LLD (honoris Causa) by Karnataka University. He was Chief Minister (1) 01-11-1956 to 19-04-1957, (2) 19-04-1957 to 16-05-1958, (3) 21-06-1962 to 03-03-1967, (4) 03-03-1967 to 29-05-1968.

- V.P. Exti Chitradurga (Karnataka).

S. R. KANTHI

Shri S. R. Kanthi was Chief Minister of Karnataka for a brief period of 09-03-1962 to 20-06-1962.

SOMANAHALLY MALLIAH KRISHNA

Son of S.C. Malliah

Somanahally, Mandya District (Karnataka) 01 May 1932.

B.A., B.L., M.C.L. (Texas).

He was Professor of International Law, Law College, Bangalore (1962-68). Minister of State for Industry – 29 January 1983 – 07 February 1984.

Finance and Commerce: 07 February – 07 September 1984. 08 September – 31 October 1984, again 04 November 31 December 1984

Chief Minister of Karnataka 11-10-1999 to 27-05-2004. Member Legislative Assembly 1962-67, 1972-77, 1989, 1999, Legislative Council 1972-77, Lok Sabha 1962-72, 1980-84, Rajya Sabha 1996-99, was Minister for Industries & Commerce, Govt. of Karnataka 1972-77. Union Minister of State for Industry during 1983-84.

At present Governor of Maharashtra.

- 28, 3rd Cross, 9th Main R.M.V. Extension, Bangalore (Karnataka).

S.R. BOMMAI

Son of Rayappa Bommai

Karadigi, Shiggaon Taluk, Dharwad District (Karnataka) 06 June 1924.

B.A., L.L.B.

Took part in Freedom Movement was member of M.N. Roy's Redical Democractic Party. Karnataka University Senate, Karnataka Liberal Education Society – elected to Assembly 1967, 1978, 1983 and 1985.

Minister for Human Resource Development – 01 June 1996 – 19 March, 1998, GoI. Elected to Rajya Sabha 1992. S.R. Bommai Sworn in as the 11th Chief Minister of Karnataka in Banglore on 13 August 1988-89.

Coal 01 – 29 June 1996.

Chief Minister of Karnataka 1988, elected to Rajya Sabha 1992, President Janata Dal 1990-96.

- 10 Lodhi Estate, New Delhi – 110 001.

VEERENDRA PATIL
Son of Basappa Patil
Chincholi Village, District Gulbarga (Karnataka)
28 February 1924-14 March, 1997.
B.A., L.L.B.

Cabinet Minister for Petroleum, Chemical and Fertilizers – 07 March – 19 October 1980.

Shipping & Transport – 19 October 1980 – 02 September 1982.

Labour & Rehabilitation – 02 September 1982 – 31 October 1984.

Industry & Company Affairs – 15 January – 24 September 1985.

Chief Minister of Karnataka 1968-71 and again was Chief Minister of Karnataka in 1989-1990.

Chief Minister of Mysore 1968-72 President Karnataka. Janata Party.

Member Rajya Sabha 1972-78; Member Delegation to U.S.S.R. 1965, to Japan and South East Asia 1970 to Australia 1972, to U.K. and Europe 1973.

- 174 – 9th Main Section Cross, Rajamahal Vilas Extension, Bangalore – 560 006.

H.D. KUMARASWAMY
Son of H.D. Deve Gowda, Former Prime Minister

He was Ramanagaram MLA in 1994. He lost the Kanakapura Assembly seat to D.K. Shivakumar of the Congress in 1999, but re-entered politics in 2004 at MLA of Ramanagaram.

46 year-old H.D. Kumaraswamy, a film producer – turned politician, is the first time MLA assumed office of Chief Minister on 3rd February, 2006 of Karnataka till date.

Kumaraswamy wins Karnataka trust vote needing 113 vote in a 224 member House, his JD(S) – BJP Govt. Polled 138 votes. Opposition Congress and others totals 66, while 10 abstained.

CHIEF MINISTERS OF KERALA

S. No.	Name of the Chief Minister	Term of Office
1.	E.M.S. Nampoothirippad	05.04.1957 to 31.07.1959
2.	Pattom Thanu Pillai	22.02.1960 to 26.09.1962
3.	R. Shankar	26.09.1962 to 10-09.1964
4.	E.M.S. Nampoothirippad	06.03.1967 to 01.11.1969
5.	C. Achutha Menon	01.11.1969 to 01.08.1970
6.	C. Achujha Menon	04.10.1970 to 25.03.1977
7.	K. Karunakaran	25.03.1977 to 25.04.1977
8.	A.K. Anthony	27.04.1977 to 27.10.1978
9.	P.K.Vasudevan Nair	29.10.1978 to 07.10.1979
10.	C.H. Muhammed Koya	12.10.1979 to 01.12.1979
11.	E.K. Nayanar	25.01.1980 to 20.10.1981
12.	K. Karunakaran	28.12.1981 to 17.03.1982
13.	K. Karunakaran	24.05.1982 to 25.03.1987
14.	E.K. Nayanar	26.03.1987 to 17.06.1991
15.	K. Karunakaran	24.06.1991 to 16.03.1995
16.	A.K. Antony	22.03.1995 to 09.05.1996
17.	E.K. Nayanar	20.05.1996 to 17.05.2001
18.	A.K. Antony	18.05.2001 to 30.08.2004
19.	Oomen Chandy.	31.08.2004 to 17.05.2006
20.	V.S. Achuthanandan	18.05.2006 to till date

KERALA

A.K. ANTONY
Son of Arakkaparambil Kurian Pillai
Sherthalay – 28 December, 1940
B.A., B.L.

Politician, General Secretary All India Congress Committee (I). Chief Minister of Kerala, 1977-78 and again 1995-96. President Kerala PCC, 1973-1977, again Chief Minister 1995 to 1996. Cabinet Minister for Civil Supplies, Consumer Affairs & Public Distribution System – 17 January 1993 – 08 February 1995, elected to Rajya Sabha in April 1985-91, and 1991-95. Travels Abroad U.S.S.R., Japan, France, U.K. and Yugosslavia. General Secretary, All India Congress Committee 1984-87. Leader of the opposition 1996 to 2001. Chief Minister from 18.05.2001 to 30.08.2004.

- "Anjanam" Ishwara Vilasam Road, Thiruvananthapuram (Kerala).

C. ACHUTHA MENON
Son of Achutha Menon
January 27, 1913, Trivandrum.
B.A., B.L.

Had distinguished academic career, started career as District Court Pleader. Joined C.P.I. 1942, WENT UNDERGROUND, 1948-52, Elected M.L.A. on communist ticket. Travancore – Cochin 1952-57; Kerala 1957-59; Finance Minister, Communist Ministry again became Chief Minister in October 1969-1977. Member Rajya Sabha 1968-69.

- Chelat House, Trichur – 4, Kerala.

C.H. MUHAMMED KOYA

He was Chief Minister of Kerala from 12.10.1979 to 01.12.1979 for a month

E.K. NAYANAR (CPM)
Kalliasseri (Kerala) 09 December, 1919-May, 2004.

He was Chief Minister of Kerla since 20 May 1994. Political worker and renowned Journalist. Joined communist movement, became an activist at the age of 20 participated in the historic "Kauur" Peasant uprising and was also associated with "Morazha" struggle against the British rule in Malabar; was arrested several times; was chief Minister 25 January 1980-20 October 1981, 26 March 1987 – 23 June 1991; leader of opposition 1982-87. Politburo Member, CPI (M); elected to Lok Sabha 1967, elected to Kerala Legislative Assembly 1974, 1980, 1982, 1987, 1991. Again Chief Minister 1996-2001

E.M.S. NAMPOOTHIRIPPAD
Son of E.M. Parameswaran Nampoothirippad and E.M. Vishnudatha Antherjanam.
Elamkulam Village, Malappuram Distt.
14 June, 1909 -1998
gave up studies in college to join civil disobedience movement 1932.

Indian Politician, Writer, General Secretary of Communist Party of India (Marxist) until 1992. Chief Minister of Asia's first elected communist Government Kerala 1957-59, 1967-69. Secretary Kerala Provincial Congress 1938-40. Congress MLA, madres 1939-40. Chief Minister Kerala 1957-59, 1967-69, elected to Kerala Legilative 1960, 1965 and 1967, 69. General Secretary C.P.I. 1962-63, detained under D.I.R., February 1, 1966 - Chief Minister of Kerala State, 1967-69. Publication, many books in Malayalam and in English : (1) India Under Congress Rule (2) Problems of National Integration. (3) Indian Planning in Crisis. Acting General Secretary India C.P. 1962-63. - Plot 10, Santhi Nagar, Trivandrum, Kerala State.

K. KARUNAKARAN
Son of Ramunni Marar
Kannur (Kerala) 05 July 1918.
Matric

Chief Minister of Kerala, came to limelight while participating in Quit India Movement, 1942. Founded INTUC Unit in Kerala and became its first President Member, Indian delegation to ILO Conference, 1957. Member Cochin Assembly 1948-49. Travancore Cochin Assembly, 1952-53 & 1954-56. Elected to Kerala Assembly in 1965, 1967, 1970, 1977 & 1980. Congress Party Chief whip 1952-53 & 1954-56. Chief Minister from 25 March 1977 to 25 April 1977. Chief Minister for Second time from 28 December 1981 to 17 March 1982. Against elected Chief Minister of Kerala in May 1982 and 1991-1995. Congress Working Committee & Parliamentary Board; AICC, since 1967.

Cabinet Minister for Industry : 10 June 1995 – 16 May 1996.

Member, AICC, CWC 1969, Congress Parliamentary Board, 1984.

- Murali Mandiram, Trissur (Kerala).

OOMEN CHANDY

1943

Career :-

Oomen Chandy like Antony, is known for his clean image and probity in Public Life. He was Home Minister in an Antony Cabinet (1981-82) and Finance Minister in aKarunakaran Ministery (1991-1994). A one time close aide of Antony. Took charge of Kerala. Chief Minister on 31 August, 2004.

He was holding the post of UDF Convenor. An Eight-time MLA from Puthupally in Kottayam district, marks the first break, from nearly three decades of congress leadership alternating between K. Karunakaran and Antony.

P.K. VASUDEVAN NAIR

Son of V.N. Kesava Pillai

Kidangoor (Kottayam Distt., Kerala) 02 March 1926.

B.A.

Joined CPI 1945; was Editor Jayayugam Daily 1954-57, elected to Lok Sabha 1957-67; Chief Minister of Kerala for a brief period in 1978-1979. Assistant Secretary Kerala State Council of CPI until 1977, Member National Council of C.P.I., Assistant Secretary, Kerala State Council of CPI, until 1977.

PATTOM THANU PILLAI
Trivandrum, July 1885.
B.A., B.L. BL from Law college Trivandrum.

made his mark as a lawyer; elected member, Travncore Legislative Assembly 1928; has been M.L.A., Tranvancore – Cochin and Kerala ever since with a short break when the state congress members were banned from contesting the seat was President Travancore state congress. Chief Minister Travancore, 1948. Chief Minister Kerala state since, February 22, 1960 to September 26, 1962.

R. SHANKAR
30 March, 1908.
B.A., B.L.

Started practice at Quilon District Court, joined the State Congress struggle, 1939; was imprisoned; General Secretary; State Congress 1940-44 was Secretary and President S.N.D.P. Yogam; nominated to the Franchise & Delimination Committee in 1946 and Reforms Committee in 1947; elected to the Travancore Legislative Assembly, 1948, was member Travancore Devaswam Board; was President K.P.C.C., Deputy Chief Minister, Kerala 1960-62; Chief Minister Kerala 1962-64.

CHIEF MINISTERS OF MADHYA PRADESH

S. No.	Name	Term of Office	
1.	Takhatmal Jalori	1950	1952
2.	Mishri Lal Gangwal	1952	April, 1955
3.	Takhat Mal Jalori	April 1952	Oct. 1956
4.	Shambhu Nath Shukla	1956	
5.	Shankar Dayal Sharma	1952	1956
6.	Ravi Shankar Shukal	01-11-1956	31-12-1956
7.	Bhagwabt Rao Annabhau Mandoli	01-01-1957	31-01-1957
8.	Kailash Nath Katju	31-01-1957	14-04-1957
9.	Kailash Nath Katju	15-04-1957	11-03-1962
10.	Bhagwabt Rao Annahau Mandoli	12-03-1962	29-09-1963
11.	Dwarka Prasad Mishra	30-09-1963	08-03-1967
12.	Dwarka Prasad Mishra	09-03-1967	29-07-1967
13.	Govind Narain Singh	30-07-1967	12-03-1969
14.	Raju Naresh Chander Singh	13-03-1969	25-03-1969
15.	shyama charan Shukla	26-03-1969	28-01-1972
16.	Prakash Chand Sethi	29-01-1972	22-03-1972
17.	Prakash Chand Sethi	23-03-1972	22-12-1975
18.	Shyama Charan Shukla	23-12-1975	29-04-1977
	President's Rule	30-04-1977	25-06-1977
19..	Kailash Chandra Joshi	26-06-1977	17-01-1978
20.	Virender Kumar Saklecha	18-01-1978	19-01-1980
21.	Sunder Lal Patwa	20-01-1980	17-02-1980
	President's Rule	18-02-1980	08-06-1980
22.	Arjun Singh	09-06-1980	10-03-1985
23.	Moti Lal Vora	11-03-1985	12-03-1985
24.	Arjun Singh	13-03-1985	13-02-1988
25.	Moti Lal Vora	14-02-1988	24-01-1989
	President's Rule	25-01-1989	08-12-1989
26.	Shyama Charan Shukla	09-12-1989	04-03-1990
27.	Sunder Lal Patwa	05-03-1990	15-12-1992
	President's Rule	16-12-1992	06-12-1993
28.	Digvijay Singh	07-12-1993	2003
29.	Uma Bharati	2003	22-08-2004
30.	Babu Lal Gaur	23-08-2004	18-11-2005
31.	Shivraj Singh Chauhan	29-11-2006	Till date

MADHYA PRADESH

ARJUN SINGH
Son of Shiv Bahadur Singh
Churhat Village, Sidhi District (MP) 05 November 1930.
B.A., L.L.B.

Vice President, Congress Party, since January 1986. He was Chief Minister of Madhya Pradesh 1980-85. Tender his resignation 23 January 1989. Elected to 9th Lok Sabha from Delhi Vidhan Sabha Member MP 1957-85. Development 1967-72. Education Minister 1972-77. leader of the Opposition, MP Assembly during Janata regime, 1977-80.

Cabinet Minister for Commerce – 15 November 1985 – 19 January 1986. Communications – 22 October 1986 – 13 February 1988. Human Resource Development – 21 June 1991 – 24 December 1994. Again Chief Minister 1985-1988.

He is Cabinet Minister of HRD in UPA government now days.

- 6 Shamala Hill, Bhopal (MP)
- 1, Race Course Road, New Delhi – 110 011.

BABULAL GAUR
1926

Former Home Minister of MP. Babulal Gaur was swarn in as successor of Uma Bharati, Chief Minister of Madhya Pradesh. He unanimously elected leader of the BJP Legislature Party at a meeting attended by party general secretaries Arun Jaitley and Shivraj Singh Chouhan on 23 August, 2004. His name was proposed by Bharati her self.

Gaur an Eight-time MLA, was minister for Local Self government in the Sunderlal Patwa regimein the early nineties. He was leader of opposition during the last phase of the congress government under Digvijay Singh.

BHAGWABTRAO ANNA-BHAU MANDOLI
December 15, 1892
B.A., L.L.B.

Practised as a Lawyer at Khandwa; has been President Municipal Committee Khandwa for three terms of five years each was member Governing Body of women Hospital Khanwa; has been member P.C.C. for the last 20 years, Chief Minister M.P. (I) 01-01-1957 to 30-01-1957 and (II) 12-06-1962 to 29-09-1963; resigned under the Kamraj Plan August 1963, Minister for Revenue, M.P. 1956-62.

DIGVIJAY SINGH
Son of Balbhadra Singh
28 February 1947.
B.A., B.Sc (Engineering)

Shri Digvijay Singh was in the royal family of Raghogarh principality, presently in Guna district of Madhya Pradesh. His father late Balbhadra Singh was former ruler of this earstwhile Indian princely state. He is an engineering graduate from G.S. Institute of Technology, Indore. He is an avid sports person with particular interst in cricket, tennis and squash.

Shri Singh joined politics at a young age of 24. Owing largely to his astute organizing and leadership qualities, he rose from within the ranks of Congress Party to become President of Madhya Pradesh Congress Committee in the year 1984 and in 1992. He distinguished himself as Minister of State and later as a Cabinet Minister in the Ministry of Shri Arjun Singh between 1980-84. Shri Digvijay Singh was elected Member of State Legislative Assembly in 1980. He was elected as a Member of Parliament in 1984 and 1991.

On December 7, 1993, he became Chief Minister of Madhya Pradesh. He has now become the longest serving Chief Minister in the history of Madhya Pradesh after winning people's mandate for the second consecutive term in the year 1998.

His mantra is participation of people in governance for sustainable socio-economic development.

Under his leadership Madhya Pradesh has bagged three prestigious international awards for development achievements. The Education Guarantee Scheme won the Gold Award of CAPAM (Commonwealth Association for Public administration and Management) at Kuala Lumpur in 1998 for universalizing access to primary education. Gyandoot project claimed the

Stockholm Challenge Award in the year 2000 for using information technology in rural areas for the direct benefit of common people. Rogi Kalyan Samiti (Patients' Welfare Society) initiative has won Global Development Network Award for breathing a new life in government run hospitals and health institutions through people's participation.

In recognition of his efforts in conserving water and soil, Shri Singh was invited to participate in the World Water Forum held at The Hague in March 2000. He was also invited to share his experiences on a panel on poverty reduction strategies held as a part of Social Summit of the UN General Assembly in Geneva in July 2000. In recognition of his innovative style of governance, he was invited to participate in the World Economic Forum held in Davos, Switzerland in January 2001.

Shri Singh is among the handful of young politicians in India, who have a vision, political will and the ability to face the challenges of the new century and to shape a better future.

DR. KAILASH NATH KATJU
Son of Tribhuwan Nath Katju
Jaora (M.P.) June 17, 1887-17 Feb. 1968.
M.A., LLD, D.Litt.

Practised at Kanpur (1908-14), joined High Court Bar, Allahabad 1914; Advocate, Allababad High Court (1921). Governor of Orissa 1947-48; West Bengal 1948-51; Minister of Home Affairs & Law, 05 November 1951 – 13 May, 1952. Home Affairs and States – 13 May 1952-09 January 1955. Defence – 01 January 1955 – 30 January, 1957. He was Chief Minister of M.P. 1957-1962.

GOVIND NARAIN SINGH
Son of Awadesh Pratap & Maharaj Kumari
Rampur Baghelan (Satna District) MP 25 July 1920.
M.A., L.L.B.

Detained for terrorist activities against British Government 1941, Jailed during Quit India Movement – 1942. Lecturer and Research Scholar Banaras Hindu University 1946. Joined IAS 1948, elected to Vindhya Pradesh Assembly 1952, Led large group of defectors against Mishra Government 1967. Chief

Minister of Madhya Pradesh 1967-69.

- E-2- 167 Arera Colony, Bhopal, Madhya Pradesh.

KAILASH CHANDRA JOSHI

Son of Uma Shankar and Rambhabai.

Hatipiplia (Devas Dist.) MP. 14 July 1929 Married Tara.

Matriculate.

President Bharatiya Janata Party MP. Formely associated with Jana Sangh was member of its MP and All India Working Committee, was Leader of Opposition in Assembly, elected to Assembly 1977. Chief Minister of MP, 1977-1978; Minister for Electricity, commerce & Industry 1978; re-elected to MP Legislative Assembly for fifth term 1980.

- 81, Mahakal Marg, P.O. Hatipilia Dewas Dist., Madhya Pradesh.

MISHRILAL GANGWAL

Samvat, Indore, 1959.

Social & Cultural work.

President of Several Social and Commercial institutions was member Indore Legislature; was Food Minister, Indore, was civil supplies Minister Madhya Bharat, commerce & Industries Minister 1949-50. Finance Minister, 1950-52 was elected leader, congress Legislature Party, Madhya Bharat Legislative Assembly 1952 was Chief Minister M.B. 1952 – April 1955.

MOTILAL VOHRA

Son of Mohalal Vora

Nagaur (Rajasthan) 20 December 1928.

Journalism

Started his career as Journalist; Vice-Chairman, M.P. State Road Transport Corporation, 1972. Minister of State for M.P. Cabinet, 1980, Cabinet Minister 1983, was President of MPCC; was Chief Minister of Madhya Pradesh; 1985, Minister of Health & Family Welfare, February 1988-89. Chief Minister of MP March 1985-89. Governor – U.P. – 1995-96.

PRAKASH CHAND SETHI

Son of Bhanwar Lal Sethi

Jhalrapatan Jhalawar District,

19 October 1920-21 February, 1996.

B.A., L.L.B.

Minister for works & Housing Govt. of India since January 14, 1980. Member A.I.C.C., 1951, M.P. Rajya Sabha 1961; re-elected 1964, to Lok Sabha 1967-71, 1979; Petroleum, Chemicals & Fertilizers – 19 October 1980 – 15 January 1982. Railway – 15 January – 02 September 1982. Home Affairs – 02 September 1982 – 19 July 1984.

Chief Minister of Madhya Pradesh 1972-75. Leader of delegation to Colombo Plan Conference Victoria 1969; Govt. of India at Commonwealth Finance International Bank of Reconstruction and Development 1969.

Awards:LLD (Honoris causa) by Vikram & Bhopal Universties. Indira Gandhi Award for National Integration on 1998. He was respected for his honesty and impartiality.

Pt. DWARKA PRASAD MISHRA
Son of Ayodhya Prasad and Janaki Devi
August 05, 1901.
B.A., L.L.B., D.Litt.

Elected to the Indian Legislative Assembly 1926, elected President Municipal Committee, Jabalpur, 1932; Appointed Minister, C.P. & Berar 1931, appointed Home Minister, M.P. Govt. 1946; Vice-Chancellor, University of Sagar 1956-63, elected leader Madhya Pradesh Legislature Congress Party September 24, 1963. Chief Minister Madhya Pradesh October 1963-67 and 09-03-1967 to 29-07-1967.
- Gour Bhawan, Civili Lines, Sagar, Bhopal, M.P.

RAJU NARESH CHANDER SINGH

He was Chief Minister of Madhya Pradesh for four days e.g. from 13.3.1969 to 25.3.1969.

RAVISHANKAR SHUKLA
Sagar, August 2, 1877.
B.A., LL.B.

Headmaster, state High School, Khairagarh for 3 years was tutor to Chiefs of Baster, Kawardha and Khairagarh, Joined Bar 1908, arrested as a non-co-operator, 1923. 2 years imprisonment and fined Rs 500, 1932, name struck off the roll of law years, 1932, but re-admitted 1935. Minister Education, July 1937, Prime Minister in the first congress Ministry, August 1938-November 1939.

Chief Minister Government of Madhya Pradesh April 1946. re-elected M.L.A. Chief Minister February 1952. Chancellor, sagar university conferred LL.D Chonoris caused by Banaras University, 1949. Chief Minister 01-11-1956 to 31-12-1956.

SHAMBHUNATH SHUKLA
1904
B.A., L.L.B., (Allahabad Univ.)

Entered Politics during the Dandi March 1932, imprisoned for Participating in the 'Quit India' movement; released, 1944; Food and Civil Supplies Minister and later Finance Minister, Rewa State 1947; nominated M.P. by the Governor-General, 1949; elected M.L.A., Vindhya Pradesh 1952. Chief Minister till October 31, 1956, elected M.L.A., M.P. 1957, 1962.

SHANKAR DAYAL SHARMA
Son of Kushi Lal and Subhadra
Bhopal, 19 August 1918-26 December, 1992.
M.A. (English Litt., Hindi, Sanskrit) Ph.D., LL.M.

He was Ninth-President of India (1992-1997). Earlier he was Chief Minister of Madhya Pradesh 1952-56. Cabinet Minister, Congress President, Vice-President 1987-1992. Member, Lok Sabha 1971-77 and Seventh Lok Sabha 1980-84. (1) Governor of Andhra Pradesh, 1984-85. (2) Governor of Punjab, 1985-86. (3) Governor of Maharashtra 1986-87.

Awards : He was chancellor of 22 universities from 1987-24 July, 1992.

SHRI SHYAMA CHARAN SHUKLA
[Indian National Congress-Mahasamund]
Pt. Ravi Shankar Shukla
Smt. Bhawani Bai
Raipur (Madhya Pradesh) 27 February 1925
B.Sc., L.L.B.

Educated at Banaras Hindu University, Varanasi (U.P.) and Nagpur University, Nagpur (Maharashtra).
Advocate, Businessman and Journalist
- Shankar Nagar, Raipur – 492 001 (MP).

Tels. (0771) 282820, 282830.

- 6, Teen Murti Lane, New Delhi – 110 011.

Tels. (011) 23792752, 23732958, 23012752

1955-77 and 1990-99 Member, Madhya Pradesh Legislative Assembly (six terms)

1967-69 : Leader of Opposition, Madhya Pradesh Legislative Assembly.

Chief Minister, Madhya Pradesh 1962-72, 1975-77. Chief Minister 1990-92. Left College to take part in Quit India Movement, 1942, remained underground. Member of Assembly 1957, 1962, 1993; Chief whip of Congress Party 1963-67. Minister 1975-77 and 1989. Leader of opposition 1990-92.

- 4, Shyama Hills, Bhopal – 462013.

SUNDAR LAL PATWA

Son of Mannalal Patwa

Kukdeshwar, Neemuch District, (M.P) 11 November 1924.

Intermediate

Minister for Rural Development – 13 October 1999 – 30 September 2000. Chemical & Fertilizers – 30 September – 07 November 2000. Mines – 08 November 2000 – 31 Augus 2001 – 31 August 2001. He was Chief Minister of Madhya Pradesh 20 January – 17 February 1980, again 5 March, 1990 to 15-12-1992.

- B-3 (74 Bungalow) Dayanand Nagar, Bhopal (MP).

TAKHATMAL JALORI

Basoda, 1895

B.A., L.L.B.

Ex-Minister for Planning, Development, Irrigation & Power Madhya Pradesh. Practised at the state Bar 1913-43; Member Working Committee Gwalior State Congress 1939, convener first meeting of Public Workers of Gwalior State, the first non-official Minister State Congress Local self Govt., Gwalior State; resigned, 1942, again appointed minister as Congress nominee, 1947. Founder Trustee, Chairman or Vice-Chairman of several educational institutions. Chief Minister Madhya Pradesh 1950-52 and April 1955-October 1956. President Madhya Pradesh P.C.C. 1953, General Secretary, A.I.C.C., New Delhi 1958-60. Chairman M.B. Land Reforms Committee 1954.

UMA BHARATI
[B.J.P.-Khajuraho (Madhya Pradesh)]
D/o Shri Gulab Singh
Tikamgarh (M.P.) May 3, 1959
6th Standard, Unmarried

Religious Missinary.

March 1988 Vice President, B.J.P., Madhya Pradesh on wards. 1989 elected to Lok Sabha (Ninth). 1991 Relected to Lok Sabha (Tenth). 1996 elected to Lok Sabha (Eleventh) 3rd Term.

Jan 1990-1992 Member, Consultative Committee under the Punjab state Legislature (Delegation of Power Acft, 1987).

1993 on wards President, B.J.P. Youth Wing.

19 March 1998. Took Oath as a State Minister in the Ministry of Human Resource Development in Central Cabinet.

2003-2004 Att Present she is Chief Minister of Madhya Pradesh, 2003 to till date. Member, Ram Janam Bhoomi Trust, engaged in V.H.P. activities. The Former Chief Minister of Madhya Pradesh is not an ordinary Politician. A gifted Public Speaker who combines the traditional and modern idiom Uma has a way of connecting with the voters, her ability to invoke religious imagery without being casteist and to link nationalism with development concerns make her unique.

Shri Vajpayee lavished Praise on Ms. Bharati calling her a devi.

At the age 5, started giving religious discourses.

By 16, she attained fame for discourses on the Ramayana.

She began traveling around thecountry to broaden her experience.

Decided early on not to marry and remain a Sadhvi, committed to Hindutva. Known as Didi to followers.

Travelled to 75 countries for her discourses.

1980 — Entered politics after coming into contact with Rajmata Vijyaraje Sindia.

1984 — First contested Lok Sabha elections from Khajuraha at 25; lost in the Post – Indira Gandhi assassination sympathy wave.

1986 — Raised her profile through the Ayodhya movement.

1988 — Became deputy chief of BJP's Madhya Pradesh State Unit.

1989 — Won Lok Sabha election from Khajuraho.

Re-elected in 1991, 1996 and 1998 ; in 1999, contested and won from Bhopal.

1992 — During demolition of Babri Masjid, she reportedly egged on Kar Sewaks saying, "Ek dhakka aur do". (she denies this).

Union Minister of state for HRD (1998 – 99), Tourism (1999 – 2000) Youth Affairs and Sports (2000 – 2002).

Coal and Mines (2002 – 2003).

2003 — Led party to big win in MP State assembly elections; was elected from Bara Malehra and became states first woman chief minister.

2004 — Summons from Karnataka court in Tiranga case led to her resignation ; she launched Tiranga Yatra. Dispute with national executive members during yatra. Se announced sanyas, but then changed her mind.

Discourses on Hindu religion and culture (since the age of six) thoughout the world.

VIRENDRA KUMAR SAKLECHA

04 March 1930.

B.A., L.L.B.

Elected to Assembly 1957, Leader Janasangh group in Assembly 1962, Deputy Chief Minister Samyukta Vidhayak Dal Government 1967, resign to take part in agitation against Kutch International Tribunal's Award, and its implementation, 1968. Deputy Chief Minister 1968-69, elected to Rajya Sabha 1972, elected to Assembly and became Chief Minister of Madhya Pradesh 18-07-1978 to 19-01-1980.

- Jawad, Mandsaur (M.P.)

SHIVRAJ SINGH CHAUHAN

Born on March 5, 1959 in Jait Village of Sehore district of Madhya Pradesh, Chauhan joined the RSS when he was only 13. M.A. in Philosophy (Gold Medalist). He took a lead in student politics and became secretary of the state wing of Akhil Bhartiya Vidyarthi Parishad (ABVP) in 1977. In 1985, he became General Secretary of the state BJYM, the BJP's Youth Wing. He was elected to the Assembly in 1990 but by the next year he took his chair in Parliament.

The OBC leader organizes a mass wedding every year in Vidisha where he gets girls from poor families married at his own expense. His immense popularity in the Vidisha – Rajgarh region made the BJP Pit Chauhan against then Chief Minister Digvijay Singh in the 2003 Assembly Elections.

The electoral battle took place in Raghogarh a seat where Singh's ancestors had been rulers for centuries, against the raja of Raghogarh, the BJP set an OBC farmer's son, Chauhan, to fight it out. Singh won the seat but Chauhan succeeded in decreasing his winning margin by more than 30,000 votes compared to the 1998 elections.

The sheer courage with which Chauhan fought the electoral battle against Singh ha seventually paved the way for his Chief Ministership. He became Chief Minister on 29.11.2005 till date.

CHIEF MINISTERS OF MAHARASHTRA

S. No.	Name	Term of Office	
1.	Y. B. Chavan	1.5.1960	19.11.1962
2.	M. S. Kannamwar	20.11.1962	24.11.1963
3.	P. K. Sawant (Caretaker)	24.11.1963	5.12.1963
4.	V.P. Naik	5.12.1963	20.2.1975
5.	S. B. Chavan	21.2.1975	17.5.1977
6.	V.D. Patil	17.5.1977	5.3.1978
7.	V.D. Patil	5.3.1978	18.7.1978
8.	S.G. Pawar	18.7.1978	17.2.1980
9.	A.R. Antulay	9.6.1980	12.1.1982
10.	B.A. Bhonsale	21.1.1982	1.2.1983
11.	V.D. Patil	2.2.1983	9.3.1985
12.	V.D. Patil	10.3.1985	1.6.1985
13.	Shivaji Rao Patil Nilangekar	3.6.1985	6.3.1986
14.	S.B. Chavan	12.3.1986	26.6.1988
15.	S.G. Pawar	26.6.1988	4.3.1990
16.	S.G. Pawar	4.3.1990	25.6.1991
17.	S.R. Naik	25.6.1991	22.2.1993
18.	S.G. Pawar	6.3.1993	14.3.1995
19.	Manohar Joshi	14.3.1995	31.1.1999
20.	Narayan Rane	1.2.1999	18.10.1999
21.	Vilasrao Deshmukh	18.10.1999	17.1.2003
22.	Sushil Kumar Shinde	18.1.2003	01.11.2004
23.	Vilasrao Deshmukh	01.04.2004	till date

No Maharashtra Chief Minister had a full term since 1975.

Sr. No.	Name of Chief Minister	Party's Name	Duration of Rle Years-Months
1.	Vilasro Deshmukh Rao	Congress	3-03
2.	Narayan Rane	Shivsena	0-09
3.	Manohar Joshi	Shivsena	3-06
4.	Sharad G. Panwar	Congress	3-00
5.	S.B. Chavan	Congress	0-09
6.	S.P. Nilangekar	Congress	0-09
7.	Vasantdada Patil	Congress	2-04
8.	B.A. Bhosale	Congress	1-01
9.	A.R. Antulay	Congress	1-06
10.	Vasantdata Patil	Congress	1-03
11.	S.B. Chavan	Congress	2-02

DATTATRAYA KASHINATH KUNTE
Son of Kashinath Woman and Godavari.
Alibag (Maharashtra) 27 October 1908.
B.A., L.L.B.

Joined civil disobedience movement, 1930, courted arrest several times; organized Rashtrate (Weekly), 1935, elected to Bombay Assembly 1946-52 re-elected to Assembly 1952, speaker 1952-56. Member Lok Sabha until 1970, President Indian National Theatres 1952-59, elected to Bombay Assembly 1937-40, 1946-56, Parliamentary Secretary to Chief Minister of Bombay 1946-52.

H.E. BAL GANGADHAR KHER
1888.
Sanskrit Scholar, B.A., LL.B.

High Commissioner for India in U.K. elected M.L.A., Bombay, from the university constituency and leader, Bombay Legislature Congress Party, March 1946; Member, constituent Assembly, 1946-50; Chief Minister Bombay, 1946-52; member council of states 1952.

M.S. KANUAMWAR

Shri M.S. Kanuamwar was Chief Minister of Maharashtra for one year e.g. from 20.1.1962 to 24.11.1963.

MANOHAR JOSHI
Son of Gajanan Joshi
Nandvi, Raigad District (Maharashtra) 02 December 1937.
M.A., L.L.B.

He was Minister for Heavy Industries and Public Enterprises – 13 October 1999. He was speaker of Lok Sabha. He was Chief Minister of Maharashtra from March 1995-99. he was Speaker of Lok Sabha. Elected to Lok Sabha' 99, Vice President Cricket Control Board of India. President Mumbai Cricket Association.

Published :- Swachh Mumbai, Harit Mumbai.

- 101, Oceana Appartments, Shivaji Park, Kaluskar Marg, Dadar, Mumbai (Maharastra).

MORARJI RANCHHODJI DESAI
Son of Ranchhodji Desai
Bhadeli Bulsar District (Gujarat)
29 February 1986-10 April 1995.
B.A., Bombay Civil Service (Resigned).

Entered provincial Civil Service of the Govt. of Bombay, 1918, resigned to join C.D. Movement, 1930; Secretary Gujarat P.C.C. 1931-37 and 1939-46. Treasurer A.I.C.C. 1950-58. Cabinet Minister for Commerce, Consumer & Heavy Industries – 14 November 1956 – 28 March 1958.

Finance – 22 March 1958 – 31 August 1963.

Chief Minister of Bombay 1952 – 56; Deputy Prime Minister & Minister for Finance 13 March 1967 – 15 July 1969. Deputy Prime Minister – 16 – 19 July, 1969. Prime Minister – 24 March 1977 – 28 July 1979 and Minister for shipping and Transport – 26 March – 14 August 1977. Home Affairs 01 July 1978 – 23 January 1979. Health & Family Welfare – 01 July 1978 – 13 January 1979. Receipient of Bharat Ratna Award – 1991.

Hon. L.L.D. (Karnataka Univ. 1957), Utkal Univ. Cuttack, 1962). Minister for Atomic Energy, Space, Electronics, Science and Technology, member Lok Sabha 1975-79. Chancellor, Gujarat Vidyapeeth Ahmedabad and Jawarharlal Nehru University; President Lok Bharati University Publication : A view of the Gita, in my view (2) A Minister and His Responsibilities (3) The Story of My Life (4) Indian Unity (5) From Dream to Reality.

NARAYAN RANE

Shri Narayan Rane was Chief Minister of Maharashtra 1.2.1999 to 18.10.1999 for 9 months (Shiv-sena).

Narayan Rane won the vote of confidence in a special session of the state assembly with a majority that has sent shock waves in the Congress camp. Surprisingly, neither the Congress-led Opposition nor the ruling Shiv Sena-BJP alliance pressed for a division of votes or debate in the confidence motion. In the normal course, the House was to deliberate on the motion for four hours, before it was put to vote. It became crystal clear at the end of the day that both the saffron-alliance and the Opposition had their own reasons to avoid the much-promised trial of strength on the floor of the House. Rane claimed that he enjoyed support of as many 183 to 184 MLAs, as against the 145 MLAs required for a simple majority in the 288-member House. Those who supported him included all the 44 independent MLAs in the House. Shiv Sena's former dissident Ganesh Naik and his two supporters, Gulab Gwande and Suresh Nawale (both former ministers of State) stayed away from the House. According to Vidhan Sabha sources, the Congress-led Opposition did not insist on voting as it would have revealed the party-wise position, a risk which the truncated Opposition could ill afford.

P. K. SAWANT

Shri P.K. Sawant became caretaker Chief Minister of Maharashtra from 24.11.1963 to 5.12.1963.

SHANKARRAO BHAORAO CHAVAN

Son of Bhaurao and Laxmibai.
Paithan (Aurangabad Distt.) Maharashtra, 14 July 1920
B.A., L.L.B.

He was Chief Minister of Maharashtra 1975-77. Again Chief Minister in 1986-88, elected to Lok Sabha 1980, 1984, Rajya Sabha 1988, 1990. Cabinet Minister for Education, Culture & Social Welfare – 19 October 1980 to 09 August 1981.

Planning – 10 August 1981 – 19 July 1984.

Defence 02 Aug. – 31 October 1984.

Again, 04 November – 31 December 1984.

Home Affairs 21 June 1991 – 16 May 1996.

Finance 25 July 1988 – 02 December 1989.

Deputy Chairman, Planning Commission 1981-84. Minister without Port Folio July 1984 – August 1984.

Chief Minister of Bombay State 1956-60.

Chief Minister of Maharashtra State 1960-62.

Deputy Prime Minister and Minister of Home Affairs 1979-80. Leader of congress Party in Rajya Sabha 1963. President Institute for Defence Studies and Analysis. Treasurer Working Committee, All India Congress 1958.

- Dhanegaon Tehisl, Nanded District, Maharashtra.

SHARAD G. PAWAR

Son of Govindarao & Shardabai.

Baramati, Pune District (Maharashtra)

12 December 1940.

B.Com.

Leader of opposition, Maharashtra Legislative Assembly, since 1980. President All India Congress Committee (S). Chief Minister of Maharashtra 1978 – 80, 1988-91, 1993-94. Minister of State for Home, Publicity, Rehabilitation and Protocol, 1972. Minister of Education & Youth Welfare, 1974. Agriculture 1975. Member, Maharashtra Legislative Assembly since 3 1967. President Maharashtra Kho-Kho Association, Kabaddi Association & Amateur Kabaddi Federation of India. Vice President, Maharashtra Wrestling Association. Minister for Defence – 26 June 1991-05 March 1993. At present Union Minister in ————————.

- House No. 42 "Ambarai" Baramati, Pune District (Maharashtra).

SHIVAJIRAO PATIL NILANGEKAR

Nilanga, (Maharashtra) 1931.

M.A., L.L.B.

Politician, Chief Minister of Maharashtra , 1985-86. President Usmanabad Dec., 1962-67, was member, Maharashtra Assembly, 1962-84 and Chairman Legislative Assurance Committee. Minister of State for Revenue, 1974-75. Appointed Minister for Public Works, Dairy Development, Animal Husbandary & Fisheries, Employment, Technical Education & Training in the Antulay Ministry, April 1977. Minister for Irrigation, Law & Hydiciary, 1983-84. Founder &

President Maharashtra Shikshan Samiti, Nilanga, Member Marathwada University Senate, since its inception. Took active Part in Hyderabad Liberation Struggle.

SUDHAKARRAO NAIK
Son of Rajusingh and Parvati
Gahuli (Pusad Maharashtra)
B.A.

Took part in Vinoba Bhave's Bhoodan movement. Minister for Dairy Development Agriculture, Animal Husbandry, Social Welfare etc. Chief Minister June 1991 – March 1993. (2) Governor of Himachal Pradesh 1994-95.

SUSHIL KUMAR. SHINDE
4th September, 1941
B.A. (Hons.), LL.B.
Agriculturist, Lawyer.

Sh. Shinde is the first Dalit Chief Minister of Maharashtra. He had to take education in a night school. He worked as a ward boy in Wadia Hospital Solapur, a peon in session court in Solapur and a Police Sub Inspector in C.I.D. for six years in Mumbai. He resigned to take up political work. He won the elections to Assembly from Solapur no less than five times consecutively. He was Minister consecutively for 18 years, during which he held almost all portfolios. As Finance Minister, he presented nine successive budgets. He was instrumental in implementing concept of Zero Based Budget. Although, Shri Shinde belongs to a Scheduled Caste Community (Dhor), he chose to contest Lok Sabha elections twice from the general constituency. Solapur, instead of from the reserved constituency and won with a big margin. He is recipient of National Citizen's Award 1993 and 1994 for his contribution in the field of Parliamentary Procedure and putting up maximum number of questions. An avid reader, Shri Shinde is a great lover of arts, classical music and drama. He has even acted in some Marathi plays and dramas. He is an eloquent orator having equal fluency in Marathi, Hindi and English.

Other Information: Receipt of National Citizen's Award 1993 and 1994 for his contribution in the fiefl of Parliamentary Procedure and Putting up maximum number of Questions; As Finance Minister of Maharashtra, presented nine successive budgets; worked at Session Court of Solapur, 1957-65; and Served as Sub-Inspector of Police C.I.D. (Intelligence), Mumbai for Six years; though belongs to Reserved Category, contested and won from General seat during 12th and 13th Lok Sabha Elections with a margin of over one lakh four thousand and seventy seven thousand votes respectively.

Books Published : (i) Vichar Vedh (Marathi)
(ii) Vichar Manthan (Hindi)
(iii) Meri Videsh Yatrayen (Hindi)

- 19, Ashok Nagar Jai-Jui Vijapur Road, Solapur-413004 (Maharashtra) Tel. : (0217) 2311039, 2312512
- 72, Dinath Court, Sir Pochkhanwala Road, Worli, Mumbai-400 025 (Maharashtra)
- 'Varsha', Malbar Hill, Bhausaheb Hiray Marg, Malabar Hill, Mumai-400 006 Tel. : (022) 23633051, 23634950 Fax : (022) 23631446

VASANT DADA PATIL
Son of Banduji Bapuji Patil
Padmala (Maharashtra)
13 November 1917 to 01 March, 1989.
Primary

Governor of Rajasthan, since 1985. Chief Minister of Maharashtra 1985 was minister of Irrigation & Power, 1972-76; became Chief Minister 1977-78. Elected to Lok Sabha from Sangli Constituency in 1980. Appointed Gen. Secretary of Congress (I) Party in 1980. Member, maharashtra Legislative Assembly 1952-67 & 1972-77 & Legislative Council 1978-79, Re-elected to legislative Assembly in 1983. Took part in individual satyagraha in 1940 for which imprisoned for six months was shot on the shoulder by Police during Quit India movement and sentenced to Byears rigorous imprisonment, released after Independence. A Pioneer of co-operative movement, in Satara and Sangli districts was Chairman, Maharashtra State Co-operative Bank & President Maharashtra Pradesh Congress Committee & Rashtriya Mill Mazodoor Sangh, Bombay. Awarded Padma Bhushan, 1965. Vasantrao Patil 71, former Maharashtra Chief Minister, Veteran Freedom Fighter and Leader of co-operative movement.

He became Chief –Minister ofs Maharashtra :

17-5-1977 to 5-3-1978,

5-3-1978 to 18-7-1978,

2-2-1983 to 9-3-1985

10-3-1985 to 1-6-1985

Governor of Rajasthan 1985 – Nov., 1987.

Award : Padma Bhushan, 1969.

VASANTRAO PHULSINGH NAIK

Gahulim Yeotmal Dist.

July 01, 1913.

B.A., L.L.B.

Deputy Minister in the old M.P. Govt. had been member Vidarbha Pradesh Congress, Director, M.P. Co-operative Centr l Bank 1951-52; elelcted M.L.A., M.P. in 1952 General elections was Deputy Chairman, M.P. Housing Board, appointed by the M.P. Govt., Minister for co-operation, Bombay, 1956-57; Member, A.I.C.C., Delegate to the International Rice, Commission and F.A.O. meetings at Tokyo (Japan), 1958. Minister for Revenue Maharashtra State, 1960-63. Chief Minister Maharashtra State, since December 5, 1963 to February 2, 1975.

VILASRAO DESHMUKH

Son of Dagdojirao and Sushilabai.

Bahaigaon (Maharashtra)

25 May 1945.

B.A., B.Sc., L.L.B.

The dynamic, popular leader with long administrative experience, organizational skill, good orator. The socio-political career of Shri Deshmukh spans over 30 eventful years during which he rose from Sarpanch of his native place, Babhalgaon to the Chief Minister of the progress State of Maharashtra.

He started social activities in his early youth. He took keen interest in drought relief work and helped the farmers.

He was elected as Director onOsmanabad District Central Cooperative Bank and also on Maharashtra State Cooperative Bank in 1979;

He entered active politics and became member of the Babhalgaon Village Panchayat from 1974 to 1979 and its Sarpanch from 1974 to 1976.

He was a member of Osmanbad Zilla Parishad and Dy. Chairman of Latur Taluka Panchayat Samiti from 1974 to 198.

As a President of Osmanabad District Youth Congress from 1975 to 1978, he worked for successful implementation of Five Point Programme of the Youth Congress.

He made special efforts to organize the youth in Osmanabad district and became President of Taluka Indian National Congress.

He was Member of the Maharashtra Legislative assembly from 1980 to 1995. During this period, as the Minister of State and the Cabinet Minister, Shri Deshmukh looked after almost all departments like Home, General Administration, Revenue, Cooperation, Public Works, Transport, Legislative Affairs, Tourism, Agriculture, Animal Husbandry, Dairy Development Fisheries, Industry, Rural Development, Education, Technical Education, Sports and Youth Welfare.

He was re-elected to the state Legislature from latur Constituency in the elections held in September, 1999.

He took oath as the Chief Minister of Maharashtra on October 18, 1999.

Shri Deshmukh had an opportunity to visit Japan, Thailand, Philippines, Taiwan and Hong Kong in 1980, to study Cooperative Movement and Agricultural Development.

He also visited West Germany, France, England, United States and Japan in 1981.

As the Chief Minister of Maharashtra, he led a official delegation in may 2000, to U.S.A. and UK and visited New York, Los Angeles, San Jose, Washington and London to interact with the investors to bring investment to Maharashtra.

From April 1995 to October 17, 1999, when he was no in Government, he kept himself engaged in expansion of his dream project. The Manjara Co-op. Sugar Mill. The Mill is computerized and well equipped with wireless system. It established a world record in 1994-95 and in 1997-98 by crushing the highest quantity of sugarcane. It has bagged 34 awards on national and international level for excellence in production and management.

Shri Deshmukh has firmly believes that education is the key to progress. He, therefore, founded the Manjra Charitable Trust which is doing commendable work. The Trust runs three colleges in latur atta and Rajiv Gandhi Institute of Technology and Sushiladevi Deshmukh vidyalaya at Airoh, Navi Mumbai.

His hobbies include reading, classical music, volleyball and table tennis. Again became Chief Minister from 1st November, 2004 to till date.

YESHWANTRAO BALWANTRAO
CHAVAN
Son of balwantrao Chavan
Deovashtrao, Sangli District (Maharashtra)
12 March, 1912-25 NOV. 1984
B.A., L.L.B.

Known as one of the builders of modern Maharashtra, Y.B. Chavan was the first Chief Minister of the State of Maharashtra when it was carved out of the erstwhile Bombay State.

When Mahatma Gandhi started the civil disobedience movement in 1930, Chavan participated in it. During his first jail term in 1932 he came in contact with the Manvendra Roy's philosophy. However, he differed with Royist views on the stand taken by them on World War and stuck with Congress Party.

He was an important volunteer in the 'Chhodo Bharat' movement of 1942 and played critical role in underground movement.

After 1952, elections he became Minister for Local Bodies and Deptt. Of Supply, later became Chief Minister of bi-lingual Bombay State and assumed the charge as Chief Minister 1960-

62 when Maharashtra became separate State.

He was called by Pandi Jawaharlal Nehru to take charge of the Defence Portfolio after Chinese War in 1962 and was Union Defence Minister between 1962-66, and later held posts as Home Minister 1966-70, Finance Minister 1970-74 and Foreign Minister in 1974 and Deputy prime Minister 1979.

He was very much influenced by Pandit Nehru who also had regard for Chavan's ability and hence had asked him to take charge of Defence Ministry which he very ably handled and boosted the morale of Forces after the Chinese war.

Y. B. Chavan can be described in brief as an efficient Minister, successful Parliamentarian and grass root leader. He was a greater orator and his speeches delivered on various occasions have been published in form of Books 'Sahyadriche Vare' (1962) 'Yugantar' (1970).

He was also an connoisseur of music, art and literature and had friends in these fields besides the friends from different political parties.

CHIEF MINISTERS OF MANIPUR
(Since Pre-independence to Union Territory Period)

S. No.	Name	Term of Office	
1.	F. F. Pearson	15.07.1947	14.08.1947
2.	M. K. Priyobrata Singh	14.08.1947	07.10.1948
3.	M. K. Priyobrata Singh	29.11.1948	15.10.1949
4.	Territorial Council	1957 – June, 1963	
5.	M. Koireng Singh	01.07.1963	12.01.1967
6.	Central Rule	12.01.1967	20.03.1967
7.	M. Koireng Singh	20.03.1967	04.10.1967
8.	Central Rule	04.10.1967	13.10.1967
9.	L. Thambou Singh	13.10.1967	25.10.1967
10.	Central Rule	25.10.1967	19.02.1969
11.	M. Koireng Singh	19.02.1969	16.10.1969
12.	President's Rule	16.10.1969	20.03.1972

S. No.	Name	Term of Office	
13.	Md. Alimuddin	20.03.1972	28.03.1973
	President's Rule	28.03.1973	04.03.1974
14.	Md. Alimuddin	04.03.1974	10.07.1974
15.	Yangmaso Shaiza	10.07.1974	06.12.1974
16.	R. K. Dorendra Singh	06.12.1974	23.07.1975
17.	R. K. Dorendra Singh	23.07.1975	15.05.1977
	President's Rule	15.05.1977	29.06.1977
18.	Yangmaso Shaiza	29.06.1977	14.11.1979
	President's Rule	14.11.1979	14.01.1980
19.	R. K. Dorendra Singh	14.01.1980	27.11.1980
20.	Rishang Keishing	27.11.1980	28.02.1981
	President's Rule	28.02.1981	19.06.1981
21.	Rishang Keishing	19.06.1981	04.01.1985
22.	Rishang Keishing	04.01.1985	04.03.1988
23.	R. K. Jaichandra Singh	04.03.1988	23.02.1990
24.	R. K. Ranbir Singh	23.02.1990	07.01.1992
	President's Rule	07.01.1992	08.04.1992
25.	R. K. Dorendra Singh	08.04.1992	31.12.1993
	President's Rule	31.12.1993	13.12.1994

S. No.	Name	Term of Office	
26.	Rishang Keishing	13.12.1994	24.02.1995
27.	Rishang Keishing	24.02.1995	16.12.1997
28.	W. Nipamacha Singh	16.12.1997	02.03.2000
29.	W. Nipamacha Singh	02.03.2000	14.02.2001
30.	Radhabinod Koijam	15.02.2001	02.06.2001
	President's Rule	02.06.2001	
	House Dissolved	07.09.2001	
31.	Okram Ibobi Singh	07.03.2002	Till date

MANIPUR

MAIRENBAM KOIRENG SINGH
December 19, 1915.
High School.

Entered active Politics as member, Nikhil Manipuri Mahasabha, a Prominent Political Party in Manipur, 1938. Joined I.N.A. (Azad Hind Fauz), 1944; Member Manipur State Legislative Assembly 1948; Member, Electoral College, Manipur 1951, President Manipur State congress Committee 1955-57; Member Manipur Territorial Council 1957-62; Chairman Manipur Territorial Council 1962-63. Chief Minister since July 1, 1963 to 12 Jan 1967 and 20-03-1967 to 04-10-1967 and 19-02-1969.

MD. ALIMUDDIN

He was Chief Minister of Manipur 02-06-1972 to 28-03-1973.

OKRAM IBOBI SINGH
S/o Sh. Okram Angoubi Singh
Thoubal Athokpam Makha Leikai, Thoubal District
19 July 1948
Graduate

Actively involved in social services since school days and became a prominent Social Worker. Took keen interest in establishing Schools, Clubs and Co-operative Society Ltd., Thoubal in 1981; Secretary, Athokpam High School and Secretary, Madhya Junior High School.

Elected to the Fourth Manipur Legislative Assembly in 1984 as Independent candidate from 35 – Khangabok Assembly Constituency, Thoubal District. Later, he joined the Indian National Congress (I) and became Chairman, Khadi & Village Industries Board from 4.11.85 to 14.1.88. Appointed Secretary, Congress (I) Legislature Party from 25.2.89 to February, 1990 during the Chief Ministership of Sh. R. K. Jaichandra Singh. Returned to the Fifth Assembly in the February, 1990 General Elections on Indian National Congress (I) ticket and became

Minister for Municipal Administration, Housing & Urban Development (MAHUD) in the R.K. Dorendra singh Ministry (8.4.1992 – 31.12.1993). Re-inducted as Minister for Industries in the Rishang Keishing Ministry (13.12.1994 – 25.2.1995).

Appointed as Vice-President, Manipur Pradesh Congress Committee (I) in 1995-96 by the AICC(I) and re-elected as Vice-President, MPCC(I) in the organizational elections held in 1997. The AICC(I) again appointed him as President, Manipur Pradesh Congress committee (I) in 1999 and was later re-elected to the same prestigious post in the organizational elections.

Returned to the Eighth Manipur Legislative Assembly in the elections held in February, 2002 and elected unanimously as Leader of the Congress Legislature Party (CLP) as well as the Congress-led Four-Party Secular Progressive Front comprising of the Indian National Congress-I (INC-I), Manipur State Congress Party (MSCP), Nationalist Congress Party (NCP) and Communist Party of India (CPI).

Became the 19th Chief Minister of the State of Manipur from March, 7, 2002 to till date.

- Thoubal Athokpam Ward No. 7, P.O. & P.S. Thoubal – 795138 (Thoubal Distt.) Manipur Tel. : 03848-22568

R.K. JAICHANDRA SINGH

Son of Rajkumar Birchandra Singh

Imphase; 9 February 1942.

M.A., L.L.B.

Joined Indian National Congress 1964, executive committee member Manipur Youth Congress 1969, Presidentm Imphase West DCC, 1971. General Secretary Manipur PCC, 1980, elected to Assembly, 1988, 1990. Minister of State for Youth Affairs & Sports 1985; for Chemicals & Petrochemicals 1985 Feb. 1988; Chief Minister 1988- February 1990. Member Rajya Sabha 1984. Manipur Bar Association, Syndicate of Manipur University 1982-84.

- Sagolbanch Road, Vijai Govind, Imphal (Manipur).

RADHA BINOD KOIJAM
Son of Shri K. Akhiljit Singh & Kamini Devi
Married Bano Angami
Imphal, 01 February, 1943
B.Sc., LL.B

He is Chief Minister of Manipur from 15 February 2001 to 02 June 2001. He was Minister Incharge of Local self Govt. & Public Works, Govt. of Manipur since Jan 1985

RAJKUMAR DORENDRA SINGH
Son of R.K. Tombisana Singh
Yamnam Leikai (Imphal) 30 September, 1934.
L.L.B.

Joined PSP, 1952, Secretary young Socialist League, 1953-54. Founder Member Manipur Nationalist Party, 1969. President MPCC 1978-80, 1989-91; took active part and imprisoned 1964 for statehood for Manipur. Speaker Legislative Assembly June-December 1974. Chief Minister 1977-77, January – November 1980, 1992-93, elected to Rajya Sabha 1988; Leader of Opposition in Assembly 1990. Receive Glory of India award 1992.
- Mairangkhom Sougaijam Kallup, Imphal.

RISHANG KEISHING
Son of Rugdi Keishing
Bungpa Khunou, 25 October 1920.
B.A.

Headmaster Christian High School Ukhrul 1949-52, Member Lok Sabha, 1952-57, 1962-67, Territorial Council 1957-62, MLA since 1972. Cabinet Minister Finance, Education, Tribal Welfare, Transport and Forest 1974-77; Chief Minister 1980-84, 1985-88, 1994-97; President Ukhrul Sub-divison Youth League, 1950-52. Executive Member Manipur Socialist Party 1949-63. President MPCC 1978, 1991-92. Member AICC, MPCC.

W. NIPAMACHA SINGH
Son of W.Gokulchand Singh.
March 1930.
B.A., LL.B. (Guwahati University)

He was a teacher and social worker. He married to Smt. Longjam Ningol Maipak Devi but, has no issues.

While a student he associated with various socio-cultural organizations and worked for economic development of the rural masses. Started his public life as an Assistant Teacher in the Johnstone High School (1960-61) and as Head Master of the Wangoi High School (1964-71). Entered into active politics in 1971 as Member of the Indian National Congress and founded various Local Clubs, Associations as well as Dramatic Institutions and Cultural Organisations. He attended the 41st CPA Conference held at Columbo in 1995 and the 10th Seminar of the CPA at London in 1996. He had also visited various countries like, Sri Lanka, erstwhile USSR, Thailand, Japan, France, United Kingdom etc.

Sh. W. Nipamacha Singh was elected to the Second and Fourth Legislative Assembly, Manipur in the General Elections held in 1974 and 1984 and was Minister of State for Education during 1977-79. Returned to Fifth Manipur Legislative Assembly in the General Elections held in February, 1990 on Indian National Congress (S) ticket and became Minister for Public Health Engineering.

Re-elected to Sixth Legislative Assembly held in February, 1995 on Congress (I) ticket and was elected as Speaker of the Manipur Legislative Assembly on 22.3.1995 and continued till 6.12.1997. He resigned from the post of Speaker on 6.12.1997 and came out of Congress (I) with 23 other Legislators including senior Ministers following political differences cropped up between him and the then Chief Minister and the break-away group of 24 Legislators formed the Manipur State Congress Party (MSCP) on 15.12.1997. Consequently, he formed the United Front (Manipur) (UFM) Ministry under his leadership with unconditional support from the Manipur Peoples Party (11), Federal Party of Manipur (3), CPI(1) and Independents (2) On 16.12.1997. He became the 11th Leader to become Chief Minister of Manipur and 7th Chief Minister after Manipur's attainment of full-fledged State on 21.01.1972.

Under his able leadership, the Manipur State Congress Party (MSCP) and its pre-poll ally, the Federal Party of Manipur (FPM) became the single largest Party securing 29 of the 58 seats for which results have been declared, in the General Elections to 7th Legislative Assembly, Manipur held in February, 2000.

Sh. W. Nipamacha Singh was unanimously re-elected leader of the United Front, Manipur for the second time on 28.2.2000 and formed the MSCP-led coalition Ministry on 2.3.2000 with unconditional support from the break-away group of 3 Members of MPP, NCP (4), each Member of JD(U) and RJD and the lone Independent Member.

- Chief Minister's Bungalow, Imphal – 795001. India.

YANGMASHO SHAIZA

15 July 1923.

He was in Manipur Civil Service, resigned 1970, elected to Manipur Assembly 1972, Minister of Finance 1972-74, formed Progressive Democratic Front, became Chief Minister July – December 1974, elected to Lok Sabha 1977, again Chief Minister 1977-79.

CHIEF MINISTERS OF MEGHALAYA

S. No.	Name	Term of Office
1.	Willamson, A. Sangama	1970-1978
2.	Brington Buhai Lyngdoh	March 1988
3.	Williamson A. Sangma	1981
4.	Flinder Anderson Khonglam	1988-1989
5.	Purno Agitok Sangma	1988-1989
6.	Salseng Chada Marak	Feb. 1993 to March 1998
7.	E.K. Mawlong	08.03.2000–14.06.2006
8.	J.D. Rymbai	15.06.2006 – 09.03.2007
9.	D.D. Lapang	10.03.2007 – Till Date

MEGHALAYA

BRINGTON BUHAI LYNGDOH
Son of Ajra Shabong & Nermai Lyngdoh
Laitlyngkot (Shillong, Assam) 02 February, 1922.
B.A., L.L.B.

He was Chief Minister since March, 1988. President Khasi Jaintia Conference, 1954-56. Vice-Chairman Council of action of All Party Hill Leaders Conference, 1960-61, elected to Assembly 1962, but resigned, re-elected, 1963. Minister for Finance & Revenue, 1970-76, re-elected to Assembly 1978, organized United Meghalaya Parliamentary Democratic Forum 1979.

Dr. D.D. LAPANG

Veteran Congress Leader D.D. Lapang was sworn in as Chief Minister of Meghalaya on 10.3.2007, ending from days of high political drama with JD Rymbai lowing out of office at the instance of the party leadership.

Governor M.M. Jacob also administered the oath of office and secrecy to 11 other ministers at hurriedly organized swearing-in ceremony at the Raj Bhawan of the 11, eight were from the congress and one each from the United Democratic Party, the Meghalaya Democratic Party, and the hun Hynniewtrep National Awakening Movement.

E.K. MAWLONG

Shri E.K. Mawlong Sworn in Meghalaya Chief Minister on 8th March, 2000. was accused of Selling the States Prime Asset, The Meghalaya House in Kolkata to a Private Company for Rittance.

FLINDER ANDERSON KHONGLAM

The six Chief Minister Flinder Anderson Khonglam, added another blot after a lottery deal was signed with a Delhi Firm flouting all norms. To day the same parties are out to "fight corruption". He was Chief Minister of Meghalaya 1988-89.

J.D. RYMBAI

Mr. Rymbai replaced Dr. Lapang as Chief Minister on June 15, 2006 when the later quit in the wake of a revolt against by party legislators.

– 16 May 1996. Lok Sabha 1977-88, General Secretary Meghalaya PCC-1976; Delegation to various International Conferences, Founder Member, National Congress Party.
- Dakopgre, P.O. Tura, West Garo Hills District (Meghalaya). India

SALSENG CHADA MARK
Son of M. Rongmuthu
Baghmara (South Garo Hills) 16 January 1941.
B.A.

Served as Head Master in High School for five years, elected to Meghalaya Assembly, 1972, 1978, 1983, 1988, 1993; Minister of State in W.A. Sangma Ministry. Minister in Lyngdoh's Ministry 1978, 1983, 1988. President Meghalaya PCC 1991. Member AICC; Chief Minister February 1993 – March 1998 .
- Gajingpara, P.O. Mehdipathar, Dist. East Garo Hills.

WILLIAMSON A SANGMA
Son of Gongsin S. Marak
Baghmara (Meghalaya), 18 October 1919.
Intermediate.

Chief Minister of Meghalaya 1970-78 and since 1981, commissioned officer in the Army, 1942-46; entered politics after world War II and later participated in Separate Hill State agitation. Founder Member Garo National Council & Its President since 1947. Founder chairman All Party Hill Leader Conference, 1961. Re-elected to Assam Assembly, 1962 (APHLC). Elected to Meghalaya Assembly, 1970 & 1973, merged with APHLC with Congress & headed 1st Congress Ministry, Delegate to UN General Assembly, 1974. Chairman State Planning Board 1979-81. Elected to Meghalaya ssembly 1983.
- Garo Hills, PO Tura; Rockside, Shilling-793 001.

J. DRINGWELL RYMBAI

He was Chief Minister from 15 June, 2006 to 9 Marcah, 2007.

Dr. D.D. LAPANG

He became Chief Minister from 10 March 2007 to till date.

CHIEF MINISTERS OF MIZORAM

S. No.	Name	Term of Office
1.	C.H. Chhunga	1972 – 1977
2.	Thenphyanga Sailo	1979
3.	Lal Thanhawla	1984-1986
4.	Lal Denga	21-08-1986 to 1987
5.	Lal Denga	1987-
6.	Lal Thanhawla	1989-1998
7.	Zoramthanga	December 1998- 3.12.2003
8.	Pu Zoramthanga	4.12.2004 – till date

MIZORAM

C.H. CHHUNGA

November 12, 1922

Played important role in the formation of Mizo Union, April, 1946; its President 1952-71; Ex-member, Autonomous Mizo-Dist. Council & Assam Legislative Assembly; Spearheaded the demand for a Separate Mizo State and headed the Coalition United Mizo Party Executive, 1971. Elected Member, Mizoram Legislative Assembly 1972. Chief Minister Union Territory of Mizoram 9 May, 1972, 11 May, 1977.

LAL DENGA

Son PU Liantlira and Pi Darchhungi

Pukpui, Lunglei District at Mizoram, 11th June, 1972.

Married to Lalbiakdiki at Aizawl on 5.11.1954.

He joined British Indian Army in 1944. Left Army in 1953. Became founder – Secretary Mizo Cultural Society in 1958.

Mizo National Famine Front was converted into a Political Party on 22nd October, 1961 and was renamed the Mizo National Front and continued his post as President. When the MNF movement was started on 1.3.1966 he went underground and led the movement till June 30, 1986 when the Peace accord was signed with the Govt. of India.

He was sworn in as Chief Minister of Mizoram interim Government on 21.8.1986.

Sh. Laldenga was elected from two constituencies Serteek and Aizạwal North II in the first Mizoram State Gneral Elections in February, 1987 and was sworn in as the First Chief Minister of Mizoram State on February, 1987.

LAL THANHAWLA

Son of H.P. Sailo & L.S. Sailo

Aizawl; 19 May 1942.

B.A.

Joined Indian National Congress 1968. President Mizoram PCC. 1973 and re-elected eight times, elected to Assembly, 1978, 1979, 1984, 1987, 1989, 1979; Chief Minister 1984-86;

1989-98. Member 9th Finance Commission, 1987-89; connected with a number a Social & Voluntary Organisations in Mizoram; President Mizoram Olympic Association. Leader of the opposition 1978-84, 1987-88.

Member, 9th Finance commission of India.

- Zarkawt, Aizawl, Mizoram.

THENPHYNGA SAILO(Brig.)
Son of Vanchheuva
Lunglei, Mizoram, 01 January 1922.

Ex-Chief Minister, Mozoram. Member Legislative Assembly Mizoram since 1978. Commissioned Officer, Defence Services 1942. Founding Officer, Assam Regiment 1944; Brigadier 1966-1974. founder & Chairman People's Conference Party. Founder Human Rights Committee, Mizoram. Received AVSM, 1972, re-elected Chief Minister in 1979, retired from Army 1974.

- Kanan Veng, Aizawl (Mizoram).

ZORAMTHANGA
Son of Darphunga and Vanhnuali
Samthang, 13 July 1944.
Graduate

Joined MNF and was its Vice-President elected to Assembly 1987,1989 was minister of Finance and Education, Government of Mizoram, Chief Minister of Mizoram from December 1998 to 3 December 2003 and again 4 December 2003 to till date.

CHIEF MINISTERS OF NAGALAND

S. No.	Name	Term of Office	
Chief Executive Councillor (Interim Body)			
	Mr. P. Shilu AO	18.02.1961	24.02.1966
Chief Ministers			
1.	P. Shilu AO	25.02.1964	14.08.1966
2.	T.N. Angami	14.08.1966	15.02.1969
3.	Hokishe Sema	16.02.1969	25.02.1974
4.	Vizol	26.02.1974	10.03.1975
5.	Jasokie	10.03.1975	20.03.1975
6.	Vizol	25.11.1977	18.04.1980
7.	S.C. Jamir	18.04.1980	04.06.1980
8.	J.B. Jasokie	05.06.1980	16.10.1982
9.	S.C. Jamir	17.10.1982	28.10.1982
10.	Hokishe Sema	29.10.1986	22.11.1987
11.	Hokishe Sema	22.11.1987	06.08.1988
12.	S.C. Jamir	25.01.1989	15.05.1990
13.	K.L. Chishi	16.05.1990	16.06.1990
14.	Vamuzo	19.06.1990	02.04.1992
15.	S.C. Jamir	22.02.1993	05.03.1998
16.	S.C. Jamir	05.03.1998	5.3.2003
17.	Neiphario	10.03.2003	Till date

NAGALAND

HOKISHE SEMA
Son of Sukiya Sema.
Apitokito (Akuluto), March 6, 1921
B.A.

He was elected member of the Interim Body and appointed as its Executive Councillor (Finance) from 1961-63. Appointed as Minister for Finance, Revenue, Medical & Public Health and Planning & Co-ordination from 1964-69. He was later appointed Governor of Himachal Pradesh in April, 1983. He was Chief Minister of Nagaland :

16.02.1969 to 25.02.1974
29.10.1986 to 21.11.1987
22.11.1987 to 06.08.1988

He was conferred the Degree of Doctor of Divinity on 7th February, 1988 by the Serampore University, Calcutta.

Founder-Leader of Youth organizations for unity and understanding among various Naga tribes, 1942-48; President Sema Students Union, 1942-58. Education Service 1952-55; Administrative Service 1956-58; member Sema Public Organisation and Naga People's Convention 1958-62, elected MLA Nagaland 1963. Minister for Finance and Health, Nagaland 1964-68. Attended the UN General Assembly in 1972 & 1976 led a delegation of the Indo-Soviet Friendship to Moscow in 1976. Became the third Chief Minister of Nagaland at the age of 48.

JOHN BOSCO JASOKIE
Son of Dr. Khosa & Uzakien
Khonoma (Nagaland) 1927
B.Sc.

Worked as Scouts & Guide for Allied Forces in World War II. Adviser to Naga National Council, organize Naga People's Convention, 1957, was Executive Council after formation of interim Body, until 1963; Member Assembly 1964-67; first Appointed Cabinet Minister after General Election in 1964, held charges of Culture & Research, Forest, Soil conservation,

Geology & Mining 1969-74. Chief Minister 1975; re-elected in 1977, was opposition Leader till April 1980, formed a new-Regional Party; was Chief Minister till October 1982, re-elected in 1982 took part in Battle of Kohima now MLA. Mr. Jasokie was appointed member of AICC soon after the NNO merged with Indian National Congress in June 1976. In 1980 resigned from congress and formed a regional party called Naga National Party (NNP). Appointed Minister Incharge of Planning in the Cabinet of Mr. Hokishe Sema.
- D-Block Kohima (Nagaland)

KIYEZHE L. CHISHI
S/o Sh. Lukashe Chishi Tribe Sema Naga
17 December, 1943.
B.A.,LL.B.

He practiced privately till appointed as Assistant Public Prosecutor in 1973 and Junior Government Advocate in 1975. Leaving his profession, Mr. Chishi joined active politics in 1976 and was elected to the Nagaland Legislative Assembly from Atoizu Constituency on U.D.F. ticket in the Fourth General Elections in 1977. He was chief minister of NPC lead coalition Government (ULP) for a short period from 15 May, 1990 to 19.06.1990.

He was re-elected in January, 1989 General Election as an NPC candidate and elected leader of the opposition. A great orator, proved his skill while participating in debates during the Assembly Sessions.

NEIPAHIR RIO
Son of Guolhulie Rio
11 November, 1950

President, Knohima District UDF Youth Wing, 1974 ; President, UDF Youth Wing, Nagaland 1976-77. Appointed Minister of Works & Housing 1993. Appointed Minister of Home, Nagaland 1998.

Democratic Alliance of Nagaland (DNA) led by the Nagaland People's Front (NPF), elelcted him as its leader.

Nagaland Governer Shyamal Dutta invited Neipahir Rio on 5-3-2003 to form the new governement. He is the fourteenth Chief Minister of Nagaland Former Chief Minister Sema elected chairman of DNA in Assembly.

Visited abroad :- Thailand, Hongkong, South Korea, Italy, France, Britain & Switzerland

P. SHILU AO
The Eldest Son of Metongchiba and Monognenla
Longjang Village in Mokokchung District
December 15, 1916-19 September 1988.
B.A., B.T.

Served in Education Department for six years. Sub-Deputy Collector 1951-53, Extra-Assistant Commissioner 1954-60. Took Prominent Part in Social Work and Political activities in Naga national Council formed at Wokha in June 1946; resigned from service and got elected as a member, Interim Body from AO area; and Subsequently to the Executive Council. Chief Executive Councillor Nagaland, March 16, 1961 – November 30, 1963. Chief Minister Nagaland, since December 1, 1963-66.

SENA CHUBATOSHI JAMIR
Son of Senayangba
Ungma (Nagaland) 17 October 1931.
B.A., L.L.B.

Previously associated with Naga National Council. Secretary Naga People's conventions; was member of Lok Sabha 1962-70. Rajya Sabha, 1987-88; Parliamentary Secretary to Minister of External Affairs, GoI, 1962. Deputy Minister for Railways, 1967 for Labour, Employment & Rehabilitation, 1967-70, for Food and Agriculture Community Development & Co-operation 1970-71; elected to Assembly 1971, 1974, 1982, 1993; Deputy Chief Minister & Minister for works, Housing Public Health, Engineering and Planning , 1977-80. Leader of opposition 1980-82 formed a new Regional Party, Member of Parliament and Member of the Indian Delegation to the United Nations in 1962. He represented Nagaland in the Commonwealth Parliamentary Association Conference at Harare, Zimbabwe in 1990. Appointed Chief Minister for the fifth time on 5 March, 1998 and is the present Chief Minister of the state. Recipient of the title of 'Lok Shree' from Institute of Economic Studies, New Delhi in 1989 and seven other awards during his political career.

He was Chief Minister :- (i) 18.04.1980 to 04.06.1980, (ii) 17.11.1982 to 28.10.1986, (iii) 25.01.1989 to 15.05.1990 & (iv) 22.02.1993 to till date.

THEPEFULO NAKHRO ANGAMI

Son of Vitse Nakhro & Vujatsumuo.

Jotsoma (Nagaland) – 1913 -7 March, 1986.

Served overseas in Indian Army, 1941 resigned and joined district administration after World War II. Chairman Angami Tribal Council 1951; Executive Member, Naga National Council 1951, resigned, 1955, helped information of Naga People Convention 1967. Speaker Legislative Assembly, 1964-66, Chief Minister 1966-69. Minister incharge of Public Works & Electricity, 1969-72.

Mr. Angami occupied a Prominent place in the public life of Nagaland on 16 August 1974. He was sworn in as a Cabinet Minister.

VAMUZO

Son of Musuhi of Yarubo Village, Phek District.

17 October, 1936 to 22.03.2000

B.A., LL.B.

Member of Assembly since 1969. Minister for Public Works 1974, was detained during Emergency. He was Chief Minister of Nagaland. 19.06.1990 to 02.04.1992. He was first elected to the State Legislative Assembly in 1969. He was re-elected in 1974. He returned from the same constituency in 1977 General Election and became a Cabinet Minister in-charge of Finance, Revenue, Industries & Commerce and Election. In 1982 General Election he again returned to the August House and was subsequently elected leader of the opposition.

- Daklane, Kohima Town.

VIZOL

Son of Notsore

Village (Kohima Dist., Nagaland) November 16, 1917.

B.A.

Served in RIAF, 1942-46 taught in School Until 1951. Principal, Naga High School, Kohima 1953-56, Vice-President Naga peoples Convention 1957-60, elected to Assembly 1964-74; was leader of opposition, 1964; Chief Minister 1974-75; 1977-80; elected to Rajya Sabha 1992, Chairman Nagaland Red Cross Society, since 1982.

He was fourth Chief Minister of Nagaland, 26.02.1974 to 09.03.1975 and 25.11.1977 to 17.04.1980.

In 1967 he was drafted to London by the Naga People to discuss their problems with Mr. Phizo, the self-exiled Naga Leader.

- 40, Asoka Road, New Delhi – 110 001.

CHIEF MINISTERS OF ORISSA

S. No.	Name	Term of Office	
1.	Dr. H. K. Mahtab	26.1.1950	12.5.1950
2.	N. K. Chaudhuri	12.5.1950	6.4.1957
3.	Dr. H. K. Mahtab	6.4.1957	25.2.1961
4.	Bijoyananda Patnaik	23.6.1961	2.10.1963
5.	Biren Mitra	2.10.1963	21.2.1965
6.	Sadasiv Tripathy	21.2.1965	8.3.1967
7.	R. N. Singh Deo	8.3.1967	9.1.1971
8.	Bishwanath Das	3.4.1971	14.6.1972
9.	Nandini Satpathy	14.6.1972	3.3.1973
10.	- do -	6.3.1974	12.12.1976
11.	Binayak Acharya	6.3.1974	12.12.1976
12.	Nilamani Routray	26.6.1977	17.2.1980
13.	J. B. Patnaik	9.6.1980	04.03.1990
14.	Biju Patnaik	5.3.1990	14.03.1995
15.	J. B. Patnaik	15.3.1995	15.2.1999
16.	Girdhar Gomang	17.2.1999	6.12.1999
17.	H. N. Biswal	6.12.1999	2.3.2000
18.	Naveen Patnaik	2.3.2000	Till date

ORISSA

B. ACHARYA

Shri Binayak Acharya was Chief Minister of Orissa during 1974-1976.

BIJOYANANDA PATNAIK
Son of Lakhinarayan Patnaik
Cuttack (Orissa) 05 March 1916-17 April, 1997.
B.Sc.

Joined the Indian National Airways and became its ace Pilot took active part in the "Quit India" movement; courted Jail for his activities in the freedom struggle; flew the Indonesian Premier Mr. Sutan Siharir to New Delhi during the Indonesian Freedom fight against the Dutch; Chief Minister, Orissa 1961-63; resigned under the "Kamraj Plan", August 1963. Cabinet Minister for steel & Mines – 26 March 1977 – 15 July 1979. Steel Mines & Coal – 28 July 1979 – 13 January 1980.

BIJU PATNAIK
Son of Lakshminarayan married Gyan.
Cuttack, March 5, 1916.
B.Sc.

His passion for flying made him leave. B.Sc. and joined the Royal Air Force. He undertook secret flying missions carrying India leaders for which he was caught in 1943 and jailed for two years. At Nehru's instance, he flew several times over Dutch Vigilance to rescue Indonesian freedom fighters. He was Chief Minister of Orissa 1961-63. Union Minister of Steel, Mines & Coal, 1977-80. Member, Orissa Assembly, 1952-67 and 1971-77. Member Rajya Sabha 1971 & Lok Sabha 1977-79; 1980-84; 1984-85. Resigned from the Lok Sabha on 25 March, 1985 and elected to Orissa Assembly from Bhubaneswar 1985. Instututed International Kalinga Prize, Monitored by UNESCO.

BIREN MITRA
November 26, 1917.
B.A.

Has been taking keen interest in the amellaration of the down trodden from his early life; was an outstanding leader of Student's movement. Courted Jail in 'Quit India' movement 1942; took active part in Labour Movement; elected to the Orissa Assembly for the third term from Cuttack City Constituency during the mid-term election, 1961. Chief Minister of Orissa since October 2, 1963 to 21 February, 1965.

BISHWANATH DAS
Ganjam District, Orissa, March, 1891
B.A., B.L.

First elected President Chhatapur Taluga Board (Ganjam) the only elected non-officail office then open to Indians in Madras. Practised in Ganjam District 1919-21. Joined Congress 1921; started Kisan Sangh in Madras Presidency, 1920; elected M.L.A. Madras Council from Ganjam District for three terms 1920-29, resigned obeying Congress call for Salt Satyagraha 1929. Courted imprisonment in the freedom Movement several times; elected congress Assembly Party 1937. Chief Minister of Orissa 1937-39; resigned on the War issue, was member, constitutent Assembly 1947-51 was member A.I.C.C. for many years – Governor of Uttar Pradesh since April 16, 1962. He was Chief Minister of Orissa 03.04.1971 to 14.06.1972.

GIRDHAR GOMANG
Son of Haribandhu
Dibririsingi (Koraput) 08 April, 1943 (Orissa).
B.A.

Member Lok Sabha since 1972. Member Orissa State Advisory Committee for Krishna – Godavari Water Dispute 1973-77. Estimates Committee 1973-74 and 1974-75. Tribal Development Agency 1972. District Development Committee 1972. Minister of State for Communications GoI July 1988-November 1989. Minister of State for Food Processing

Industries 1991-92 for Programme implementation and Planning 1993 September 1995 for Mines Sept. 1995 – May 1996. Chief Minister of Orissa 06.02.1999-06.12.1999.

H.N. BISWAL

Shri H. N. Biswal was Chief Minister of Orissa during 6.12.1999 to 2.3.2000.

HAREKRUSHNA MAHTAB (DR.)

Son of Krishna Das, Foster Child of Jagannath Mehtab.
Agarpara, Balasore District (Orissa)
21 November 1899-2 January, 1987.
Revenshaw College, Cuttack, D. Litt., LLD

Ex-Deputy Leader of the congress in Parliament, elected M.L.A., of Bihar and Orissa 1924. Courted Jail several times in the freedom movement; President Utkal P.C.C., 1930 and 1937, member congress Working Committee, 1938-46. (1) Orissa Chief Minister 1946-50. (2) Chief Minister of Orissa 26.01.1950 to 12.05.1950 & 1957-61. (3) Governor of Bombay 1955-56. Cabinet Minister for Industry & Supply – 12 May – 26 December 1950. Commerce & Industry – 26 December 1950 – 13 May 1952 was conferred Honorary Degree Doctor of Literature by the Andhra University in 1950.

JANAKI BALLAV PATNAIK

Son of Gokulanand & Rambha
Rameswar Village, District Puri (Orissa)
03 January 1927.
B.A. (Hons), M.A.

Chief Minister of Orissa since 1990 was Member, Lok Sabha, 1980. Sub-Editor, Editor, Eastern Times 1949. Deputy Minister for Defence – 05 February 1973 – 23 December 1976. Minister of State for Defence – 23 December 1976 – 24 March 1977. Cabinet Minister for Tourism & Civil Aviation – 14 January – 06 June 1980. Lok Sabha 1971-77; Chief Minister of Orissa December 1980-1990, 1995-99.

- Paurusha, Tulsipur, Cuttack (Orissa).

NABAKRUSHNA CHAUDHURI
Son of Late Gokulananda Chaudhuri
Cuttack, 1901.
Santiniketan. Took to Agriculture – 1927.

Joined Mahatma Gandhi Sabarmati Ashram in 1923-24; established Congress Solialist Party in Orissa 1934; Prominent Leader in Orissa of states people movement ; was in prison during 1942 movement, was secretary, Orissa P.C.C.

Joined the C.D. Movement and led a movement for non-payment of Chowkidary Tax in Balasore District; 1930. appointed minister, Orissa 1946 Chief Minister of Orissa 1950-1957.

NANDINI SATPATHY
Daughter of Kalindi Charan Panigrahi
Cuttack, 19 June 1931.
M.A.

Chief Minister of Orissa 1972-73 and 1974-77. Deputy Minister without portfolio attached to t he Prime Minister – 14 February 1969 – 26 June 1970. Minister of State for Information & Broadcasting – 26 June 1970 – 14 June 1972. President Orissa Pradesh Congress Committee & Secretary Orissa Women's Relief Commission, Paris. Resigned from congress, 1977, with Jagjivan Ram to form congress for Democracy, which later merged into Janata Party, Chairman Children's Film Society of India.

Deputy Minister attached to Prime Minister 1969-70, Leader Indian Film delegation to Moscow 1966, 1968 and Tashkents 1972. General Conference UNESCO, Paris 1972. Member Indian delegation to commonwealth session UN, New York 1970.
- 107, Surya Nagar, Bhubaneswar – 751 003 (Orissa).

NAVEEN PATNAIK
Son of Bijoy Anand Patnaik
Cuttack (Orissa) 16 October 1946.
B.A.

1997 – Elected to 11th Lok Sabha.
Member, Committee on Commerce
Member, Library Committee
Member, Consultative Committee,

Ministry of Steel and Mines.

1998 – Founder President, Biju Janata Dal

1998 – Re-elected to 12th Jok Sabha (2nd term)

Leader, B.J.D. in Lok Sabha

1998-99 – Union Cabinet Minister, Steel and Mines

1998-99 Memebr, General Purposes Committee

1999 – Re-elected to 13th Lok Sabha (3rd term)

13 Oct., 1999 – Union Cabinet Minister, Mines & Minerals

2000 – Elected as Member, Orissa State Legislative Assembly from Hinjili Assembly Constituency.

Book published :

(i) A Second Paradise

(ii) A Desert Kingdom; and

(iii) The Garden of Life

Literary, Artistic and Scientific Accomplishments

Writes articles on culture and environment.

Social and Cultural Activities

Founder Member, Indian National Trust for Art and Cultural Heritage (INTACH)

Special Interests

Culture and Environment

Favourite Pastime and Recration

Reading, watching programmes on culture, history and environment.

Countries visited

Widely traveled

Other Information

Played a pioneering role in the international recognition of Indian Design; and worked for handloom weavers to enlarge home market for Indian textiles.

Chief Minister, Orissa from 5.3.2000 to till date.

NILAMONI ROUTRAY

Son of Chandrasekhar Routray

Mukundapur (Balasore Dist. Orissa) 24 May 1920.

B.A., L.L.B.

Took part in freedom struggle at the age of 12 years was one of the founders of All India Student's Federation Orissa. Courted arrest several times. He was editor of daily Prajatantra. Member

Assembly 1948-67, 1971-73 and 1977. Member Rajya Sabha 1975-77; Chief Minister Orissa 1977-80. Cabinet Minster for Health & Family Welfare – 05 December 1989 – 23 April, 1990. Environment & Forests – 23 April – 10 November 1990.

- Cuttack Chandi, Cuttack (Orissa).

RAJENDRA NARAYAN SINGH DEO

Seraikela, March 31, 1912.

B.A.

He was Maharaja of Patna State since February 1933 was member of Chamber of Princes and Vice-President Council of Rulers of the Eastern States Agency, was Chief patron, 5th All Indian Cultural unity conference, formed a new party called Ganatantra Parishad, 1949, which merged with the Swatantra Party after the 1962 Parliamentary election; was elected to the Lok Sabha, 1952; elected M.L.A., Orissa since 1957, Leader of the opposition in the Assembly 1957-59. Deputy Leader and Finance Minister, was Chief Minister of Orissa March 1967 – January 1971.

SADASIV TRIPATHY

Shri Sadasiv Tripathy was Chief Minister of Orissa State during 1965-1967.

CHIEF MINISTERS OF PUNJAB

S. No.	Name	Term of Office	
1.	Dr. Gopichand Bhargava	15.8.1947	13.4.1949
2.	Lala Bhim Sen Sachar	14.4.1949	18.10.1949
3.	Dr Gopichand Bhargava	19.10.1949	20.06.1951
	President Rule	20.6.1951 to 17.4.1952	
4.	Lala Bhim Sen Sachar	17.4.1952	20.06.1953
5.	Dr. Gopichand Bhargava	22.6.1953	6.7.1954
6.	Lala Bhim Sen Sachar	7.7.1954	23.1.1956
7.	S. Pratap Singh Kairon	24.1.1956	21.6.1964
	President's Rules	21.6.1964	6.7.1964
8.	Ram Kishan	6.7.1964	5.7.1966
	President's Rule	5.7.1966	31.10.1966
9.	Gurmukh Singh Musafar	1.11.1966	8.3.1967
10.	Justice Gurnam Singh	9.3.1967	24.11.1967
11.	S. Lakshman Singh Gill	24.11.1967	23.8.1968
	President's Rule	23.8.1968	17.2.1969
12.	Justice Gurnam Singh	17.2.1969	26.3.1970
13.	S. Prakash Singh Badal	26.3.1970	14.6.1971
	President's Rule	14.6.1971	16.3.1972
14.	Gyani Zail Singh	17.3.1972	30.4.1977
	President's Rule	30.4.1977	19.6.1977
15.	S. Prakash Singh Badal	19.6.1977	17.2.1980
	President's Rule	17.2.1980	7.6.1980
16.	S. Darbara Singh	7.6.1980	7.10.1983
	President's Rule	7.10.1983	29.9.1985
17.	S. Surjit Singh Barnala	29.9.1985	11.5.1987
	President's Rule	11.5.1987	25.2.1992
18.	S. Beant Singh	25.2.1992	31.8.1995
19.	S. Harcharan Singh Brar	8.9.1995	21.11.1996
20.	Smt. Rajinder Kaur Bhattal	22.11.1996	21.2.1997
21.	S. Prakash Singh Badal	12.2.1997	24.2.2002
22.	Capt. Amarinder Singh	27.2.2002	Nov. 2006
23.	Parkash Singh Badal	11.04.2006	Till date

PUNJAB

CAPTAIN AMARINDER SINGH
Son of Late Yadavindra Singh of Patiala
Patiala, 11 March, 1942.
Lawrance School Sanawar 1950 to 1952.
The Doon School 1953-1959
Joined the National Defence Academy, 1959
Graduate from there December, 1962.

Joined the Indian Military Academy, Dehradun January, 1963. Commissioned in the Indian Army, June, 1963. Posted to 2nd Bn. The Sikh Regt. (Both his father and grand father has served with this Battalion)

Served in Field Area – Indo Tibetan Border for 2 years with this Battalion. Appointed Aide-De-Camp to Lt. General Harbaksh Singh, VRC. GOC-in-Cwestern Command.

Resigned from the Army in early 1965 as his father (Late Maharaja Yadavindra Singh) was appointed Indian Ambassador to Italy and he was required at home.

But he rejoined the Army again immediately hostilities broke out with Pakistan and took part in the actual operations in the "War against Pakistan and again resigned after the war was over in early, 1966.

Married Preneet Kaur, D/o S.Gyan Singh Kahlon, ICS (Then Chief Secretary, Holland France and Iran)

7th Jan. 1980 – Elected Member of Parilament (Lok Sabha)

10th June, 1984 – Resigned Membership of Parilament and from the Congress (I) as a protest against the Army entry in Darbar Sahib's Complex.

5th Feb., 1985 – Convenor, The Sikh Forum.

23 Aug., 1985 – Joined Shiromani Akali Dal. 27th Sept., 1985 – Elected Member Legislative Assembly, Punjab

30th Sept., 1985 – Became Cabinet Minister, Punjab Agriculture, Forests, Rural Development and Panchayats

2nd May, 1986 – Resigned from the Cabinet, as a protest against the entry of Para-military forces and police in Darbar Sahib's Complex.

5th May, 1986 – elected Leader Legislature Party, Shiromani

Akali Dal, Punjab Vidha Sabha remained till the State Assembly was dissolved in April, 1988.

May 1988 – Member of the Working Committee of Shiromani Akali Dal.

May 1991 – Formed a new party, Shiromani Akali Dal (Panthik) and elected Convenor of this party.

Jan., 1992 Shiromani Akali Dal (Panthik) and SAD Longowal merged and Elected Chairman, Parliamentary Board, SAD.

5 Feb., 1992 – Elected unopposed MLA from Samana Constituency.

19, Oct., 1995 – Elected Chairman of the Committee of World Wide Fund for Nature-India, for the Punjab, Himachal Pradesh and Union Territory, Chandigarh.

Feb., 1997 – Resigned from SAD and revived the Shiromani Akali Dal (Panthik) and elected its Chairman.

12 Sept., 1997 – Shiromani Akali Dal (Panthik) merged with Indian National Congress.

4th July, 1998 – Appointed President Punjab Pradesh Congress Committee (I)

10th Oct., 1998 – Elected Chairman INTACH for 3 years.

25th Nov., 2000 – Elected President Punjab Pradesh Congress Committee (I) At present he is Chief Minister of Punjab from 27.02.2003 to till date.

BEANT SINGH

Village Bilaspur of Ludhiana Distt. (19.2.1922)

B.A., Govt. College, Lahore

He joined Army in the year 1943 and served there for two years. He started his public career as a social worker in 1945, after leaving the Army.

After partition of the country he settled at Village Kotli, about 5 kms. From Doraha in District Ludhiana.

He started his political career in 1950, was elected Chairman Block Samiti, Doraha in 1960. He was elected Director of Central Cooperative Bank, Ludhiana in 1963.

He was elected to Punjab Vidhan Sabha from Payal Constitutency in 1969 as an Independent Candidate with the support of the Congress Party and was re-elected from this constituency in 1972 and 1977. He remained Member of the Estimate Committee, Public Accounts Committee, Committee on

Welfare of Scheduled Scastes, Scheduled Tribes and Backward Classes and Committee on Subordinate Legislation, Remained Chairman of Privileges Committee, Chairman of Estimates Committee twice.

In 1977 when India was in the grip of Janta Wave, he was again elected on the Congress ticket from the same constituency and was elected General Secretary of Opposition i.e. Congress Lagislature Party. He remained President of the District Congress Committee (Rural) Ludhaiana from 1977 to 1980.

In 1980 he was re-elected to Punjab Vidhan Sabha and become a Minister in the ministry headed to Punjab Vidhan Sabha and became a Minister in the ministry headed by Sh. Darbara Singh. He held the portfolios of Revenue, PWD and Technical Education and did a commendable work in these Departments.

In 1985 he was made the General Secretary of the Punjab Pradesh Congress Committee (I). Later on keeping in view his service to the party he was appointed the President of the Punjab Pradesh Congress committee (I) in March 1986.

In 1991 Organisational Elections he has been elected President unanimously to head the Punjab Pradesh Congress (I) as a President of PPCC he traveled day and night throughout the state of Punjab and led a campaign against the Terrorism. He was the only political leader who visited almost every village affected by the terrorist violence.

In February 1992 elections Congress party in Punjab won with 85 seats. He was unanimously elected leader of the Congress (I) legislature party and sowrn in as the Chief Minister of the State after six years of the President's Rule. i.e. 25.02.1992 to 31.08.1995.

Under his leadership the state has entered in the new phase of history. The terrorism has been brought under the control. Peace has set in.

He has completely restored democracy in the state by completing elections of Municipal Committees and Panchayats.

A new ear has begun where there is trust, respect and complete harmony. Punjab is back to its glorious place.

BHIM SEN SACHAR
December 01, 1893.
B.A., L.L.B.

High Commissioner for India in Ceylon, joined N.C. Movement 1921; Secretary Punjab P.C.C. 1921. Municipal Commissioner Gujaranwala 1924-33, elected M.L.A. Punjab on Congress Ticket 1936-47. Finance Minister Punjab Government, 1946-47; elected member constituent Assembly of Pakistan from West Punjab in 1947 and Deputy Leader of the Congress Party; Leader Congress Legislative Party Punjab, India 1949; Governor of Orissa 1956-57; Governor of Andhra Pradesh 1959-62. Chief Minister of Punjab State as under :-

(1) 14.04.1949 to 18.10.1949.
(2) 17.04.1952 to 20.06.1953.
(3) 07.07.1954 to 23.01.1956.

DARBARA SINGH
Son of Dalip Sing & Bishan Kaur
Jandiala (Punjab) 10 February 1916.
B.A.

Politician, Congress (I) Member Rajya Sabha April 1984. Congress (I) Parliamentary Board 1984. Former Chief Minister of Punjab, 1980-83. Member of Lok Sabha, 1971-77. Minister for co-operation & consolidation of Holdings, Punjab Govt. 1956-57. Agriculture & Panchayati Raj, 1962-64; Home 1964-66, President PCC 1961-64.
- Jandiala, Phillaur Tehsil, Jalandhar Punjab.

GOPI CHAND BHARGAVA

Sh. Gopi Chand Bhargava was Chief Minister of Punjab state during the period as follows :

(1) From 1947 to 1949
(2) From 1949 to 1951
(3) From 1953 to 1954

GURMUKH SINGH MUSAFIR
Attock Distt. (Punjab) January 1899
Giani

He was President, East Punjab Congress Committee 1949. Member A.I.C.C. suffered imprisonment for participating in Congress Movement 1930 and 1942.

He was Chief Minister Punjab 1966-67. Member Executive Congress Party in Parliament since 1952. Took active part in Akali Movement Jathedar Akal Takht, General Secretary S.G.P.C. and Shiromani Akali Dal. Devoted to Poetry & Journalism. Join Congress in 1923, Chairman, Reception Committee 61st Session of the Indian National Congress, Member Delegation to Stockholm Peace Conference, 1954. Visited Japan, Russia.

(JUSTICE) GURNAM SINGH
25 February, 1899
B.A., Barrister-at-Law.

Started Legal Practice at Lyallpur; elected President Bar Association 1946 and 1947; Started Practice at the Punjab High Court Simla, 1949; Judge PEPSU High Court 1950-1956 and Punjab High Court 1956-59, entered Politics 1962, Chief Minister Panjab 1967-68 and 1969-70.

H.No. 286, Sector 10-A, Chandigarh

HARCHARAN SINGH BRAR
Son of Balwant Singh
Sarainaga Village (Faridkot Dist. Punjab) 22 Jan. 1922.
B.A. (Lahore).

He was member, Punjab Assembly, 1957-72; Minister for Irrigation & Power, Punjab Govt. 1962-65, later incharge of Sports and Civil Aviation. He was President of Ferozepore District Congress Committee, Deputy Leader of Congress Legislature Party, General Secretary of Punjab PCC. Chief Minister of Punjab 08.09.1995 to 21.11.1996. (2) Appointed Governor of Orissa, September 1977. (3) Governor of Haryana 1977-80.

Sarainaga, P.O. BARIWALA, Dist. Faridkot (Punjab).

LAKSHMAN SINGH GILL

Shri Lakshman Singh Gill was Chief Minister of Punjab state 24.11.1967 to 23.8.1968.

PARTAP SINGH KAIRON
Kairon Village, Amritsar 1901.

M.A. (Michigan). Educated Khalsa College, Amritsar.

Started Political career in America by actively associating with the Ghaddar Prty working for India's Liberation from foreign rules; joined congress 1929, imprisoned for five year, 1932 CD Movement; led the Kisan agitation, 1938; General Secretary Punjab Provincial Congress Committee 1939-46; elected President P.C.C. 1950-52. Member Congress working Committee 1946-53 and 1958; elected M.L.A. Punjab 1937 re-elected 1945; elected member constituent Assembly 1946, re-elected M.L.A. 1952, 1957 and 1962. Minister 1947-49. Development Minister 1952-56. Chief Minister of Punjab State January 1956-June 1964.

PRAKASH SINGH BADAL
Son of Raghuraj Singh
Abul-Kharana Village, Faridkot Dist. (Punjab)
08 December 1927.
B.A. : Ed. At Formans' Christian College, Lahore

Entered politics in 1947; elected M.L.A. for the first time in 1957; again elected to the Punjab Vidhan Sabha in mid-term polls held in 1969 and thereafter in 1972 on Sant Dal Akali ticket; remained Development Minister in 1969 and Chief Minister from 27th March, 1970 to 14th June, 1971; founder of Guru Nanak College for Women, Mukatsar and Guru Gobind Singh College for Men, Gidderbaha; remained Chairman, Block Samiti Lambi; remained Sarpanch of Gram Panchayat, Badal; Member of the working committee of the Shiromani akali Dal; remained Senior Vice-President of Shiromani Akali Dal; Chairman, Parliamentary Board of the Shiromai Akiali Dal; Member of the Working committee of the Shiromani Gurdwara Prabandhak Committee; remained Leader of the Opposition in the Punjab Vidhan Sabha from 1972 to July, 1975; remained confined in Karnal Jail from Ist June, 1973 to 12th June, 1973 in connection with Civil Liberties Morcha at Karnal; detained under MISA during Emergency from 9th July, 1975 to 19th January, 1977; got schools opened and took active part in promoting educational and health schemes in the constituency; rendered service for the welfare of the Society; elected to the Lok Sabha from the Faridkot Parliamentary Constituency in

March, 1977; remained Union Minister for Agriculture and Irrigation from 26th March, 1977 to 17th June, 1977; elected M.L.A. in 1977; remained Chief Minister Punjab from 20th June, 1977 to 17th February, 1980; again elected to the Vidhan Sabha in 1980 and in 1985 from Gidderbaha. He was Leader of Oppositino in the 8th Punjab Vidhan Sabha. In the just concluded election (Feb. 1997); he contested from Quila Raipur and won by 11022 votes from his nearest rival.

Agriculture

Member, Chelmsford Club, New Delhi

Social Service

- Vill. Rge and P.O. Dada, Distt. Faridkot, 256, Sector 9, Chandigarh. Ph. : 0172-43744

Re-elected Chief Minister in November 2006.

RAM KISHAN

Son of Shri Ram Chand.

Jhang Dist. West Pakistan 1913.

Matric

Left College to join the freedom struggle in the wake of the death of Lala Lajpat Rai 1929 is a staunch congressman; courted Jail for six years during the independence Movement, elected commission, Lahore Municipal Corporation 1946, elected MLA Punjab from Jullundar constituency, 1952-57. Municipal Commissioner Jullandar City 1948-51. Deputy Minister Punjab 1956-57, member A.I.C.C. became a minister of state, Punjab 1962. He was President, District Congress Committee, Jullundur 1948-52, General Secretary, Punjab Pradesh Congress for several years. Member Punjab Legislative Assembly 1952-1957 to 1962-1967; Deputy Minister Punjab Govt., Chief Minister Punjab 1964-1966.

Smt. RAJINDER KAUR BHATTAL

Daughter of S. Hira Singh Bhattal

Lahore (Paksitan) 30.9.1945

B.A., B.Ed. at Sangrur

Belongs to the family of Freedom Fighters and born in Central Jail (Lahore).

Remained chairperson of Social Welfare Advisory Board, Punjab 1988-1990. Secretary Khadi & Village Industries Board 1972-1977.

Remained in Jail for two months for Protesting against the arrest of Smt. Indira Gandhi in 1979. Elected to Punjab Vidhan Sabha in 1980 and became Minister of State for Tourism, Cultural Affairs and Archeology till 1983. Elected M.L.A. in 1992 and became Cabinet Minister was elected President of Punjab Pradesh Congress Committee on 9.5.1997. Chief Minister of Punjab state w.e.f. 21.11.1996 to 11.2.1997. At present she is Deputy Chief Minister of Punjab.
- V&PO Lehra, The. Sunam, Distt. Sangrur.

SURJIT SINGH BARNALA
Son of Nar Singh
Ateli Begpur, Distt. Mohindergarh, Haryana. October 21, 1921
B.A., L.L.B. (Lucknow University)

He participated in the Quit India Movement as a university student suffered lathi blows and was arrested.

Mr. Barnala started law partice in Nabha state and shifted to Barnala after partition. He contested election of the State Assembly on Akali Dal ticket in 1967 successfully. Since then he has been representing the Barnala Constituency in one form or the other and his name became synomimous with the town. He became Education Minister in Punjab in 1969. During Emergency he was in jail for 14 months. In 1977 he was elected to the Lok Sabha and served as Agriculture, food and irrigation minister in Janta Govt. headed by Shri Morarji Desai from 1977 to 1979.

Mr. Barnala was again elected as MLA in 1980. After the assassination of Sant Longowalji he was elected as President of Shiromani Akali Dal in 1985. He became Chief Minister of Punjab after a landslide victory of Akali Dal in 1985 Assembly elections. This was a difficult period of militancy in Punjab and his efforts to fight militancy were praised by the Prime Minister Shri Rajiv Gandhi in the Parliament and the President also lauded his services while addressing both the Houses of Parliament. His Govt. was dismissed on 11.5.1987.

Mr. Barnala was appointed Governor of Tamil Nadu in 1990. He did not agree to recommend dismissal of the duly elected Government in the State having a large majority in the Assembly. The Central Government wanted to transfer him to Bihar as Governor but Mr. Barnala resigned from Governorship.

In 1996 he was elected as member of Lok Sabha again and is leader of Akali Dal group in Lok Sabha. In 1998 Lok Sabha Elections has again been elected from Sangrur in Punjab. He has also been sworn in as Cabinet Minister.

ZAIL SINGH
Son of Kishan Singh
Sandhwan Village, Faridkot District (Punjab)
05 May 1916 – 25 December, 1994.
Private Education.

President of India since 25 July 1982-87. Union Home Minister, 1980-82. Chief Minister of Punjab, 1972-77. Member, Rajya Sabha 1956-62; Punjab Assembly 1962 & 1972-77; & Lok Sabha 1980 from Hoshiarpur. Founder Faridkot State Congress. Member, AICC, 1948-49. A Veteran freedom fighter was minister (State and Central). Founded Faridkot State Congress; launched national flag movement, 1946, formed a parallel Government in Faridkot State 1948. President State Praja Mandal, 1946-48. President PCC, 1962-72. President Punjab Co-operative Union Minister of Home Affairs January 1980.

PRAKASH SINGH BADAL
Son of Raghuraj Singh
Abul-Kharana Village, Faridkot (District) Punjab
December 8, 1927 (Shares the date with Sonia Gandhi)

Ist time MLA 1957 (from Malout on Congress ticket) has fought about 15 elections and represented Lambi, Gidderbaha, and Malout.

Shiromani Akali Dal President is all set to become Chief Minister of Punjab for the fourth time. In a political career that spans almost five decades, the Octogenarion Akali leader had earlier ascended to the coveted office in 1969, 1977 and 2002.

1st time CM March 27, (1970 to June 14, 1971)
2nd time CM June 20, 1977 to Feb. 17, 1980
3rd time CM February 1997 to February, 2002.
Leader of opposition, In 1972, 1980 and 2002.

At the Center : Has been an MP and Union Minister of agriculture and irrigation in the Morarji Desai Government in 1977.

Agitations : Was jailed in Karnal in connection with civil liberties agitations, under MISA during Emergency.

His credentials came under doubt during terrorism, and went into hibernation.

Bada political journey started with Atal Behari Vajpayee in 1957. And in the same year that former Prime Minister Jawahar Lal Nehru landed a young Vajpayee, telling him he would lead the country someday, Giani Kartar Singh who was revenue minister in Punjab then, predicted bigger things for Badal.

Re-elected Chief Minister from November 2006 to till date.
Badal Village, Muktsar Tehsil, Faridkot District (Punjab)

CHIEF MINISTERS OF RAJASTHAN

S. No.	Name	Term of Office
1.	Dr. Mohan Sinha Mehta	1944-1947
2.	Suraj Mal Chaudhari	1947-48
3.	Gokul Bhai Daulat Ram Bhatt	1948-49
4.	Hira Lal Dev Pura	
5.	Cadambi Seshachar Venkatachar	January to April 1951
6.	Tika Ram Paliwal	Six Months (1952)
7.	Jai Narayan Vyas	Nov. 1952 – Nov. 1954
8.	Mohan Lal Sukhadia	1954 – 1971
9.	Sobha Ram	
10.	Hari Deo Joshi	1973 – 1977
11.	Bhairon Singh Shekhawat	1977 – 1979
12.	Jagannath Prasad Pahadia	1980 – 1981
13.	Shiv Charan Mathur	1981 – 1985
14.	Shiv Charan Mathur	1988 – 1989
15.	Bhairon Singh Shekhawat	1990 – 1998
16.	Ashok Gehlot	1998 – 2003
17.	Vasundhara Raje Scindia	2003 – till date

RAJASTHAN

ASHOK GEHLOT
Son of Lachhman Sing Gehlot
Mahamandir, Jodhpur District (Rajasthan). 3 May, 1951
B.Sc., M.A., L.L.B.

Politician, Member of Parliament since 1980. President Pradesh Congress Committee (I) Rajasthan since September 1985. Member Public Accounts Committee, 1980-82. General Secretary, Pradesh Congress Committee (I) 1982. Deputy Minister for Tourism – 02 September 1982-14 February 1983. Sport 07 February – 31 October 1984 again 12 November – 31 December 1984. Textile (Independent Charge) – 21 June 1991-17 January 1993. He was Chief Minister of Rajasthan December 1998 to 2003.

- Mahamandir, Jodhpur (Rajasthan).

BHAIRON SINGH SHEKHAWAT
Son of Devi Singh was Sub-Inspector of police, Sikar State.
Khachowriawas (Sikar Dist. Rajasthan) 23 October 1923.
M.A.

Former Rajasthan Chief Minister Bhairon Singh Shekhawat was regarded with some favour. He has long experience in Public Life. He was Chief Minister of Rajasthan since 1990. He was Sub-Inspector of Police, Sikar State, Member, State Assembly since 1952 except 1974-77. Member Rajya Sabha 1974-77 was President Rajasthan Janasangh 1953-60; 1963-64, Vice-President All India Janasangh 1966; was detained during Emergency; member national Executive of janata patry.

The National Democratic Alliance (NDA) nominee and former Rajasthan Chief Minister Bhairon Singh Shekhawat become the country's 12th Vice-President on 12 August 2002, defeating the Joint Opposition candidate Sushil Kumar Shinde by an impressive 149 votes.

Shekhawat began his career as Policeman As a COP, he

arrest Shaitan Singh notorious decoit of the Shekhawat region. For this bravery medal was given to him by the ruller of Sikar. He served the state in three innings as Chief Minister.l No other leader in the state perhaps enjoy such a large following as he does. On 19 August 2002 Bhairon Singh Shekhawat was sworn in the 12th Vice President of India by President A.P.J. Abdul Kalam. He has been Chief Minister of Rajasthan three times, 1977–1978, 1990–1998 polled 454 of the 766 votes caste by MPs on August 12, Shinde got a disappointing 305 votes.

CADAMBI SESHACHAR VENKATACHAR
Son of C. Seshachar
July11, 1899
B.A., I.C.S., C.I.E., O.B.E.

Entered Indian civil service by open competition in London and Posted to U.P., 1923. Served in Political Department of Government of India in Various capacities at Rajkot, Baroda and Indore, 1927-33. Rural Development commissioner U.P. 1935-37. member constituent Assembly of India, 1947-48. Chief Minister, Rajasthan January to April 1951.

GOKULBHAI DAULATRAM BHATT
Son of Daulatram Ramji
Hathal, Sirohi, Rajasthan 1899.
St. Xaviers college, Bombay.

Left Studies to join Non-Co-operation movement 1919. Chairman, Reception Committee, Jaipur congress; Political Adviser and Chief Minister Sirohi State, 1948-49; courted Jail several times; occupied High Positions in congress.

HARIDEO JOSHI
Son of Pannalal and Kamala Devi
Khandu (Banswara Dist. Rajasthan); 17 December 1921.

Took active part in Political movements, 1942-46; President Rajsthan PCC 1952; member Assembly, 1952-77 & since 1980. Chief Whips of Congress party 1957-63; Chief Minister, 1973-77, Chief Editor Navyug, Jaipur.

HEERA LAL DEVPURA
Son of Chhagan Lal & Chand Bai
Kabwara (Udaipur Distt. Rajasthan); 12 October 1925.
B.Sc., L.L.B.

Took Part in Quit India Movement and suffered imprisonment 1942; President land Mortgage Bank, 1962; elected to Assembly, 1967; Minister of State for Public Relations and Tourism, Rajasthan Government 1967-77 for Irrigation 1973-77, was General Secretary Rajasthan PCC (I) 1978-80. Member in February 1985 after the resignation of Mathur, Speaker Assembly 1985-89.

- Gayatri Sadan, Sawai Jai Singh Highway, Jaipur.

JAGANNATH PRASAD PAHADIA
Son of Nathi Lal
Bhusawar Village, Bharatpur District (Raj.) 15 January 1982.
M.A., LL.B.

Member Lok Sabha 1957-62, 1962-77, Rajya Sabha 1965, re-elected 1966, Deputy Minister of Finance 13 November 1967 – 17 October 1969.

Agriculture 02 May 1971 – 22 July 1972. Communication – 22 July 1972 – 23 December 1976. Labour 23 December 1976 – 14 March 1977. Minister of State for Finance – 14 January – 05 June 1980. Chief Minister of Rajasthan 1980 to 1981.

- VPO Bhusawar, Bharatpur Dist. Rajasthan.

JAINARAYAN VYAS
Jodhpur, 1898.
Had his early education locally.

M.P. Ex-Chief Minister Rajasthan from November 1952 – November 1954.Joined the Congress; organized the Marwar Peasant Movement; courted Jail five times for Political activities; externed form Jodhpur State for many years; settled in Bombay and turned to Political Journalism editing the Akhand Bharat; elected General Secretary, All India States People conference 1939-49; Chief Minister first Popular Ministry, Jodhpur 1948; was President Rajasthan P.C.C., was Minister, Rajasthan.

MOHAN SINHA MEHTA (DR.)
Bhilwara (Rajasthan) April 20, 1895.
M.A., LL.B, Ph.D (London).

Vice-Chancellor, Rajasthan University since 4 January 1960. he was secretary and later Vice-President All India Seva Samiti, Allahabad. Diwan, Baswan state, 1937-40. Revenue and Education on Minister, 1941; Chief Minister 1944-47; Member, central advisory Board of Education; Meawar State. Indian Ambassador to Netherlands till June 1951. High Commissioner in Pakistan 1951-55.

MOHANLAL SHUKADIA
S/o Sh. Purshottamdas
Nathdwara (Udaipur) July 31, 1916.
L.E.E. (Bombay)

Entered politics during 'Quit India Movement'; Minister for Civil Supplies, P.W.D. Relief and Rehabilitation, Mewar State; became Development Minister when the state of Rajasthan was first formed; elected to the Legislative Assembly April 25 1951 – March 3, 1952. Chief Minister Rajasthan since November 13, 1954-71. Governor of Karnataka 1972-75. Governor of Andhra Pradesh 1975-76. Governor of Tamil Nadu 1976-77.

PANDIT HIRALAL SHASHTRI
Jaipur, November 24, 1899.
Sahitya Shastri, B.A.

Member of Lok Sabha from Sawai Madhopur (Rajasthan). General secretary. All India States People's conference; member Constituent Assembly of India; first Popular Chief Minister, Jaipur State and then Rajasthan State.

SHIV CHARAN MATHUR
Son of Durga Prasad and Damyanti Devi
Madhi-Kanungo (Guna Dist. M.P.) 14 February 1926.
B.A., Dip. In LW Mumbai.

Chairman Bhilwara Municipal Board 1958-59. Pramukh Bhilwara Zila Parishad, 1961-64. Member Lok Sabha 1964-67 and since 1991. Assembly 1967-72, 1972-77, 1980-85, 1985–90. Minister of Education 1967 for Power 1968, for Education 1969-

71, for Power 1971-72; for Agriculture Food & Civil Supplies 1973-77. Chief Minister Rajasthan 1981-85, 1988-89; Chairman Public Undertaking Committee. Member Executive Committee Commonwealth Parliamentary Association.

- 5-D, Institutional Area, Jhalana Dungri, Jaipur.

SHOBHA RAM

M.A., LL.B.

Ex-Revenue Minister, United State of Rajasthan; Treasurer Rajasthan P.C.C. Gave up legal Practice and Joined active Politics, 1942 observed 17 days fast in sympathy with Mahatama Gandhi member Rajputana Regionel council; Council of the India states People's conference, 1946-47 and 1947-48. Adviser to the Alwar state Government and subsequently Chief Minister, United State of Matsya.

SURAJ MAL CHAUDHARI

01 January 1901

B.A., LL.B.

Minister for Public works, Punjab since August 18, 1958. Practised at the Hissar bar, till April 1957 was President District Bar Association for six years elected member & Vice-Chairman, District Board, Hissar 1928; elected M.L.A., Punjab, 1937 had been Parliamentary secretary; undivided Punjab; Dewan, Chief Minister, Bharatpur State, 1947-48. Member Punjab Legislature till 1954; Minister for Health, consolidation, Panchayats and co-operation, Punjab, April 16, 1957-August 18, 1958.

TIKARAM PALIWAL

01 July 1909.

B.A., L.L.B.

Took part in Salt Satyagraha, 1930, courted arrest several times in freedom movement; was Chief Minister of Rajasthan for six months, 1952; member Lok Sabha, 1962-67; President Rajasthan Unit of Janata party 1977.

- Diggi House, Jaipur.

VASUNDHARA RAJE SCINDIA
D/o Sh. Jivaji Rao Scindia
Bombay, Maharashtra, 1953
B.A. (Hons.) (Eco & Pol. Science), Bombay University.
Married to Hemant Singh, 1972.

Vice president, Yuva Morcha, BJP, Rajasthan 1987-92 for two years.

1989 Elected to Lok Sabha (Ninth)

1991 Re-Elected to Lok Sabha (Tenth)

Elected to Lok Sabha (Eleventh)

1998 Re-elected to Lok Sabha (Twelveth)

1999 Re-elected to 13th Lok Sabha (5th Term)

1990 Member, (i) Legislative Assembly, Rajasthan for 5 years (ii) Library Committee, March 27, 1990 and Consultative Committee ministry of Commerce and Tourism, 1990.

1991-96 (iii) Consulatative Committee, Ministry of Power, Science of Technology.

1998-99 Minister of State for External Affairs-19 March, 1998 to 13 Octobber, 1999.

13 October, 1999 on wards :- Union Minister of State (Independent Charge), Small Scale Industries and Agro & Rural Industries, Department of Personnel and Training, Department of Pernsions and Pensioners Welfare in the Ministry of Personnel, Public Grievances and Pensions; Department of Atomic Energy and Departmnet of Space.

At present she is Chief Minister of Rajasthan from 2003 to till date. She talks about a corruption-free administration and development strategy. She won against Rejesh Pilot's wife, Rama Pilot from Jhalraptan in Jhalawar district. BJP won absolute majority in Rajasthan. After all, she's created a miracle.

CHIEF MINISTERS OF SIKKIM

S. No.	Name	Term of Office	
		From	To
1.	Kazi Lhendup Dorjee Khangrarpa	1974	1979
2.	Nar Bahadur Bhandari	1979	1984
3.	B.B. Gurung	May 11, 1984	May 24, 1984
4.	Nar Bahadur Bhandari	1985	1994
5.	Sanchaman Limboo	May 18, 1994	Dec. 11, 1994
6.	Pawan Chamling	1994	Till date

SIKKIM

B.B. GURUNG
Son of Bharat Dhoj
Chaking Village (Sikkim); 11 October 1929.
B.A.

Joined Sikkim State Congress 1956. Its General Secretary until 1966, elected to Assembly 1967, was executive Councillor, incharge of Education, Forest & Transport, re-elected to Assembly 1974, General Secretary, AICC 1975-77, Speaker of Assembly 1977-79. Leader of Opposition in Sikkim Assembly Attended commonwealth Parliamentary Association Conference at Sri Lanka 1982. Political Adviser of Chief Minister since 1994. Joined AICC (I) 1983. Minister of Finance Sikkim Govt. 1983. Chief Minister of Sikkim, 11 May 1984-25 May 1984.
- Zongri, Jorethang – 737 121.

KAZI LHENDUP DORJEE KHANGSARPA
Pakyong, East Sikkim, 1904

He was the first chief Minister of Sikkim State. In 1953 he became President of Sikkim State Congress and held that post till 1958. He was Chief Minister from 1974 to 1979.

Former Sikkim Chief Minister Kazi Lhendup Dorjee was conferred with 'Padma Vibhushan' Award on 26th January 2003 for his Service to the nation.

NAR BAHADUR BHANDARI
Son of Balaram & Chandemaya
Malbansey Busty, Soreong Bazar (Sikkim) 05 October 1940.
M.A.

Appointed Primary Teacher in Chakhung School 1968, resigned from service 1974. He was put house under arrest from 1974 to 1976 and latter kept in Sikkim Central and Behrampur Jail in West Bengal under 'MISA' from 1976 to 1977. Joint politics formed Sikkim Janata Parishad Party and contested elections 1979; formed Sikkim Sangram Parishad 1984 and elected to Lok Sabha and Assembly 1985, re-elected to assembly 1989; Chief Minister 1985-89, 1990 May-1994. Member Sikkim Legislative Assembly, 1979-84.

- Tashiling Secretariat, Gangtok – 737 191.

PAWAN KUMAR CHAMLING

Son of Ash Bahadur & Dhan Maya

Yangang (South Sikkim); 22 September 1950.

Matriculation.

Entered in Politics, 1974. Vice-President District Youth Congress 1975, General Secretary & Vice-President Sikkim Prajatantra Congress 1978; elected to Legislative Assembly 1985; Minister for Industries, Information and Public Relation's in Nar Bahadur Bhandari Minister. Chief Minister of Sikkim since 1994 till date. Pride of India Award 1999-. Best citizen of India 1999 to till date. Secular India Harmony Award 1998. Manavseva Puraskar, 1999.

SANCHAMAN LIMBOO

Son of Man Singh and B.M. Subba.

Hee Yangthang, West Sikkim; 15 January 1949.

B.A., B.T.

Served as teacher and Assistant Education Officer Education Department of Sikkim Government for 12 years. Joined Sikkim Janata Parishad Party 1979, elected and inducted in Cabinet and entrusted with portfolios of Industry, Health and Education & again in March 1985. Joined Sikkim Sangram Parishad 1984; Fourth Chief Minister, May 1994-December 1994.

CHIEF MINISTERS OF TAMIL NADU

S. No.	Name	Term of Office
1.	O.P. Ramaswamy Reddiar	20.3. 1947 to 1949
2.	P.S. Kumaraswamy Raja	7.4. 1949 to 1952
3.	Rajagopalachari Chakravarti	10.4. 1952 to 1954
4.	K. Kamraj	13.4. 1954 to 2.10.1963
5.	M. Bakthavachalam	3.10. 1963 to 1967
6.	C.N. Annadurai	6.3. 1967 to 1968
7.	V.R. Nedunchezhian	3.2. 1968 to 1969
8.	M. Karunanidhi	10.2. 1969 to 31.1. 1976
9.	President's Rule	1.2. 1976 to 29.6. 1977
10.	M.G. Ramachandran	30.6. 1977 to 16.2.1980
11.	President's Rule	17.2. 1980 to 8.6. 1980
12.	M.G. Ramachandran	9.6. 1980 to 24.12. 1987
13.	V.R. Nedunchezhian	24.12. 1987 to 1988
14.	Smt. Janaki Ramachandran	7.1. 1988 to 29.1.1991
15.	President's Rule	30.1. 1988 to 26.1. 1989
16.	M. Karunanidhi	27.1. 1989 to 1990
17.	President's Rule	30.1. 1991 to 23.6. 1991
18.	Smt. J. Jayalalitha	24.6. 1991 to 12.5. 1996
19.	M. Karunanidhi	13.5. 1996 to 14.5.2001
20.	Smt. J. Jayalalitha	15.5.2001 to 21.9.2001
21.	O. Pannerselvam	21.9.2001 to 2003
22.	J. Jayalalitha	2003 to 12.05.2006
23.	K.M. Karunanidhi	13.5.2006 to till date

TAMIL NADU

C.N. ANNADURAI
(1909-1969)

He was Founder of DMK (Dravida Munnetra Kazhagam) Former Chief Minister of Tamil Nadu. The most popular Chief Minister of Tamil Nadu 1969 and eminent Writer in Tamil. His Political Guru an eminent writer in Tamil E.V. Ramaswamy.

Smt. JANAKI RAMACHANDRAN

Janaki Ramachandran, Wife of late MG Ramachandran, is Sworn in as Chief Minister of Tamil Nadu on 7 January 1988.

Smt. JAYARAM JAYALALITHA
Daughter of R. Jayaram
Mysore City, 24 February, 1948.
Matric

Under the guidance of her mentor Puratchi Thalaivar Dr. M.G.R. She entered into Politics in 1982 and became a Member in AIADMK. In January 1983 she was appointed as the Propaganda Secretary of AIADMK. In February 1983, she was sent on her first election campaign by Dr. M.G.R. when he asked her to canvass votes for the AIADMK candidate in the Tiruchendur Assembly Constituency bye-election. She succeeded in the election campaign and made astounding victory for the Paty candidate against all odds. In 1984 she was elected as a Member of Parliament to the Rajya Sabha and retained the seat until she was elected to the Tamil Nadu Legislative Assembly in 1989.

When Dr. M.G.R. fell ill and was under medical treatment in U.S.A. the AIADMK had to fight the General Elections to the Lok Sabha and Tamil Nadu Legislative Assembly in December 1984. In Dr. M.G.R.'s absence she took his place and worked for the massive victory for AIADMK and Congress (I) alliance. After the demise of Dr. M.G.R. in 1987, the AIADMK Party split into two factions. As the General Secretary of the Party she contested to Tamil Nadu Legislative Assembly in January 1989 and was elected from Bodinayakkanur. She became the first

Woman Leader of Opposition of Tamil Nadu Legislative Assembly. In February 1989, the two factions of the AIADMK reunted under her leadership and she was unanimously elected as the General Secretary of the unified AIADMK.

In 1989 she restored the 'Two Leaves' election symbol to her Party. In 1989 General Election to the Lok Sabha, she steered the AIADMK. Congress (I) alliance to a historic victory in Tamil Nadu and Pondicherry.

Thereafter she secured victories in all the subsequent bye-elections to Tamil Nadu Legislative Assembly from Marungapuri, Madurai East and Pernamallur Assembly Constituencies.

Won a remarkable victory by contesting in both Bargur and Kangeyan Constituencies during the General Election held in 1991; Moreover, she is the cause for the massive Victory of her party and alliance by winning 225 Constituencies out of 234. Subsequently, she resigned the Kangeyam Assembly seat she had won, then made her party candidate contest in that Constituency and made him secure an astounding Victory.

Further, she is the cause for the 100 per cent Victory of her party and alliance in Tamil Nadu and Pondicherry in the election to 40 Lok Sabha Constituencies held at the same time. Now, Chief Minister.

- 'Veda Nilayam', 36, Poes Garden, Madras-600 086.
Ph. : Off. : 562345, Res. : 459594

KUMARASWAMI KAMRAJ
(1903-1975)

Leader of the Indian Ntional movement; President, Indian National Congress 1963, earlier Chief Minister Tamil Nadu (1954-63). Sponsored the : Kamaraj Plan" for revitalizing the Congress Organization, resigned under this plan for party work, October 2, 1963. President, Indian national Congress 1963-68; visited USSR, Bulgaria, Hungary, East Germany and Yugoslavia. Awarded Bharat Ratna Posthumously in 1976. He was Chief Minister of Tamil Nadu 1954-1963.

M. BAKTHAVACHALAM
1897
B.A., L.L.B.

Gave up practice at the Bar, 1927 – was connected with India a Tamil daily; Deputy Mayor Madras Corporation, 1936 was member and Vice-President, Chingleput District Board for six years from 1932; Vice President Tamil Nadu Congress Committee Bharat Sevak Samaj, 1935; acted as Secretary, Tamil Nadu Congress Committee for numbers of years; Member All India Congress Committee; Public works Minister Madras 1946-52. Convenor Bharat Sewak Samaj. Minister of Agriculture & Community Projects, Madras 1953-54; Minister for Home 1957-62. Minister for Finance 1962-63. Chief Minister, Madras since October 1963.

M. KARUNANIDHI
Son of Muthuvel and Anjuham
Tirukuvalai (TN) 03 June 1924.
High School.

President Dravida Munetra Kazhagam, since 1969, and Ex-Chief Minister of Tamil Nadu, Member of Tamil Nadu Assembly since 1957. Minister of Public Works, Tamil Nadu Govt. 1967-69. Deputy leader of DMP Party in Assembly 1962-67. Founded Dravida Munnetra Kazhagam with Annadurai and others in 1949. Popular Play-wright and Poet. Widely known as Kalaignar : Written Scripts for Several Tamil films. 'Chief Minister Tamil Nadu 1969-76; 1989-90; elected to Assembly 1977. Legislative Council 1983.

Award : D. Litt. (Hon.) by Annamalai University 1971.
- 7-AS, Gopalapuram IV St. Madras-600086.

M.G. RAMACHANDRAN
Kandy (Sri Lanka) 17 January 1917-1987.
Primary School Education

Chief Minister of Tamil Nadu 1977-80 and 1980-84. He remained the Chief Minister of Tamil Nadu until his death winning three consecutive elections. Popular Tamil matinee idol for over three decades. Actor, film producer & director was treasurer of DMK and Vice-Chairman of small savings in Tamil Nadu. Member, Tamil Nadu Assembly, since 1967. Member DMK for 20 years founded AIADMK in 1972. His newly founded party having won majority in 1977 polls forms ministry.

Assembly dissolved in 1980. His Party (AIADMK)obtained majority in Assembly elections again the same year. Foreign Travels : Burma, Japan, U.S.S.R., U.K. etc.

Award : Recipient of Bharat Ratna 1988.

O. P. RAMASWAMY REDDIAR

Sh. O. P. Ramaswamy Reddiar was Chief Minister of Tamil Nadu 20.3.1947.

O. PANNER SELVAM

Sh. O. Panner Selvam was Chief Minister of Tamil Nadu 21.9.2001 to 2003.

P.S. KUMARASWAMI RAJA

Son of Late Jagga Raja.

Rajapalayam, Ramnad Dist., June 1898

Early Education in Rajapalayam.

Has closely Associated himself with the congress movement since 1920. elected Leader, Madras congress Legislature Party March 1949. Chief Minister, Madras State 1949-52.

RAJA GOPALACHARI CHAKRAVARTI

Son of Chakravarti Venkatarya Iyengar.

Thorapalli Village, Salem district (TN);

10 December 1878-25 December, 1972.

B.A., L.L.B.

Cabinet Minister without portfolio – 15 July – 25 December 1950. Home Affairs – 26 December 1950 – 05 November 1951. Chief Minister of Madras1952 to 1954 . First and last Indian Governor General of India 1948-50, known as Rajaji. Recipient of Bharat Ratna, 1954, Founder of Swatantra Party 1959. First and last Indian Governor – General of India during 1948-50.

V. R. NEDUNCHEZHIAN

Shri V. R. Neduchezhian was Chief Minister of Madras state 24.12.1987 to 1988.

CHIEF MINISTERS OF TRIPURA

S. No.	Name	Term of Office
1.	Sachindra Lal Singha	1963-1972
2.	Samir Ranjan Barman	1973-1978
3.	Nripen Chakraborty	1978-1988
4.	Sudhir Ranjan Muzumdar	February, 1988-1998
5.	Manik Sarkar	March 1998-till date

TRIPURA

MANIK SARKAR

He was Chief Minister Tripura March 1998 to till date.

NRIPEN CHAKRABORTY

Left Studies at the call of Gandhiji.

MLA, Participated in Civil Disobedience Movement. Joined CPI, 1935 also joined congress, Socialist party led by the JP; Joint Secretary Congress Socialist Party Bengal, 1936-39, Chief Minister 1978-88; Leader of opposition, 1988.

Expired 26 December, 2004.

- Tripura Legislative Assembly, Agartala.

SACHINDRA LAL SINGHA

Son of Dindayal & Bilash Monjurl.

Agartala, 07 August 1907.

Vitoria College.

Took part in freedom struggle and against monarchy in Tripura, suffered imprisonment several times, was extended from Tripura for revolutionary activities. Chairman Territorial council 1957; Chief Minister of Tripura 1963-72; Member Lok Sabha 1977-79. Advisory Board for Tripura.

SAMIR RANJAN BARMAN

Son of Sudhir Ranjan and Renu Bala

Kishore Ganj, Distt. Bangladesh, 28 April, 1940

B.A., LL.B.

Joined Agartala Bar as an advocate, 1963, later joined Indian National Congress; elected to Assembly 1972; appointed Minister in Coalition Govt. 1977 Minister for Home, Law 1986. General Secretary Tripura PCC 1980; Member Bar Council of India.

Chief Minister of Tripura 1973 – 78.

SUDHIR RANJAN MAJUMDER
Son of Ananda Mazumdar.
Gagra Village (Comilla Dist. Bangladesh) 18 May
M.A., B.Ed.

General Secretary Youth Congress Committee, Tripura Working President Tripura INTUC 1982-87. Chairman Tripura PCC 1987-89, elected to Assembly 1988. Chief Minister Tripura State February 1988 –1998

CHIEF MINISTERS OF UTTAR PRADESH

S. No.	Name	Term of Office	
1.	Gobind Ballabh Pant	1.4.1946	27.12.1954
2.	Dr. Smpurnand	28.12.1954	6.12.1960
3.	Chandra Bhanu Gupta	7.12.1960	1.10.1963
4.	Smt. Sucheta Kripalani	2.10.1963	13.3.1967
5.	Chandra Bhanu Gupta	14.3.1967	2.4.1967
6.	Charan Singh Choudhuri	3.4.1967	25.2.1968
7.	President's Rule	25.2.1968	25.2.1969
8.	Chandra Bhanu Gupta	26.2.1969	17.2.1970
9.	Charan Singh Choudhuri	17.2.1970	1.10.1970
10.	President's Rule	2.10.1970	18.10.1970
11.	Tribhuvan Narayan Singh	18.10.1970	4.4.1971
12.	Kamala Pati Tripathi	4.4.1971	12.6.1973
13.	President's Rule	12.6.1973	8.11.1973
14.	Hemwati Nandan Bahuguna	8.11.1973	30.11.1975
15.	President's Rule	30.11.1975	21.1.1976
16.	Narayan Datt Tiwari	21.1.1976	30.4.1977
17.	President's Rule	30.4.1977	22.6.1977
18.	Ram Naresh Yadav	23.6.1977	28.2.1979
19.	Banarsi Das	28.2.1979	17.2.1980
20.	President's Rule	17.2.1980	9.6.1980
21.	Vishwanath Pratap Singh	9.6.1980	19.7.1982
22.	Shripati Misra	19.7.1982	3.8.1984
23.	Narayan Datt Tiwari	3.8.1984	23.9.1985
24.	Vir Bahadur Singh	24.9.1985	24.6.1988
25.	Narayan Datt Tiwari	25.6.1988	5.12.1989
26.	Mulayam Singh Yadav	5.12.1989	24.6.1991
27.	Kalyan Singh Yadav	24.6.1991	6.12.1992
28.	President's Rule	6.12.1992	4.12.1993
29.	Mulayam Singh Yadav	4.12.1993	3.6.1995
30.	Kumari Mayawati	3.6.1995	17.10.1995
31.	President's Rule	18.10.1995	17.10.1996
32.	President's Rule	17.10.1996	21.3.1997
33.	Kumari Mayawati	21.3.1997	21.9.1997
34.	Kalyan Singh	21.9.1997	12.11.1999

35.	Ram Prakash Gupta	12.11.1999	28.10.2000
36.	Rajnath Singh	28.10.2000	8.3.2002
37.	President's Rule	8.3.2002	3.5.2002
38.	Kumari Mayawati	3.5.20002	29.8.2003
39.	Mulayam Singh Yadav	29.8.2003	
40.	Mayawati	2007	Till Date

UTTAR PRADESH

BANARSIDAS
Son of Ramjeelal & Gulabdevi
Uteaali (Bulandshahr Dist. UP); 8 July 1912.

Took part in Freedom Struggle, suffered imprisonment several times was President of UPCC 1970-73; first elected to Assembly 1946, re-elected 1952, 1962, 1967, elected to Rajya Sabha 1972; was Parliamentary Secretary Uttar Pradesh Govt. elected to Lok Sabha 1983, visited Jamica, U.S., London, Rome, Cairo etc. Chief Minister of Uttar Pradesh 28.2.1979 to 17.2.1980.

BASHIR HUSSAIN ZAIDI (Col.)
Son of Shaukat Hussain
Delhi, 30, July 1898.

Served in Aligarh University 1923-30, entered Rampur State Service, 30. Minister Rampur State 1930-36, Chief Minister 1937-49. Member Constituent Assembly 1947-49, Provisional Parliament 1949-51, Lok Sabha 1952-57, Rajya Sabha 1964-70. Vice-Chancellor Aligarh Muslim University 1956-62, member executive council Jamia Milia. Padma Vibhushan 1976.

CHANDRA BHANU GUPTA
Son of Late Shri Hiralal
UP, 14 July 1902.
M.A ., L.L.B. Lucknow University.

Politician, practiced Law 1925, member UPCC and AICC since 1926. Jailed in Freedom Movement Lucknow University; 1927, Member AICC 1926-59, (Vice President 1958. M.L.A. UP 1937-62. Chief Minister UP, 1960-63; resigned under the "Kamaraj Plan", August 1963. Chief Minister UP March 1967 and 1969. Leader of the opposition in UP Legislative Assembly 1967-68. Chief Minister of UP 1960-62, 1962-63, 1967, 1969-70. Leader Congress Legislative Party (Opposition) 1970-74. Chief Minister

U.P. 1946-47. Food and Civil Supply Minister, U.P. Government, 1947.
- Seva Kuti, Pan Dariba, Lucknow, Uttar Pradesh, India.

CHARAN SINGH (CHOUDHURI)
Son of Meer Singh & Gayatri Devi
Noorpur Village, Meerut District (UP);
23 December 1902-29 May 1987
B.Sc., M.A., L.L.B.

Vice Chairman, District Board Meerut 1930-35, Member Uttar Pradesh Legislative Assembly, 1937-39 and 1946-77; Parliamentary Secretary, Uttar Pradesh, 1946-51; leader of the opposition, Uttar Pradesh Legsilative Assembly, 1971-77; Member, (i) Sixth Lok Sabha, 1977-1979 and (ii) Seventh Lok Sabha 1980-1984.

Former Prime Minister of India 1979-80. Elected to Lok Sabha, 1980 as Janata (S) member from Baghpat, UP. Associated with Congress 1929-67. Founder Leader, Bharatiya Kranti Dal, 1967; Bharatiya Lok Dal 1974. Janata Party 1977; Lok Dal 1979. Chief Minister of UP, 1967-68 and February, 1970; Cabinet Minister for Home Affairs – 26 March 1977-30 June 1978.

Deputy Prime Minister during Janata regime and Minister for Finance – 24 January – 16 July 1979. Prime Minister and Minister of Home – 28 July 1979 – 13 January 1980 was Chairman of Bharatiya Kranti Dal 1964-67. President, DMKP; publications :-

(1) Abolition of Zamindari;
(2) Co-operative Farming X-rayed.
(3) India's Poverty and its solution,
(4) Indian Economy – A Gandhian Blueprint.
(5) Economic Night-mare of India; Its cause and Cure.

GOBIND BALLABH PANT
Son of Monarth pant
Almora (Uttaranchal)
(10 September 1887-7 March, 1961)
B.A., L.L.B.

Cabinet Minister without Portfolio – 03-10 January 1955. Home Affairs 10 January 1955 – till death. Heavy Industries – 30 August – 0 14 Nove 1956. Freedom fighter, Chief Minister of UP 01-04-1946 to 27-12-1954. Recipient of Bharat Ratna Award 1957. Abolished Zamindari.

HEMWATI NANDAN BAHUGUNA
Son of Rewati Nandan Bahuguna
Bughani Village, Garhwal District (Uttaranchal)
25 April 1919-17 March, 1989
Married Kamala.
B.A.

Took part in Quit India Movement in 1942. Member U.P. Congress Committee from 1952 and All India Congress Committee, 1963-69. Minister of state for communications – 02 May 1971 – 7 November 1973. Cabinet Minister for Petroleum, Chemical & Fertilizers – 28 March 1977 – 15 July 1979. Finance – 28 July – 19 October 1979. Chief Minister, U.P. 1973-75. Member AICC 1957, & on its Working Committee, 1959-71; its General Secretary 1969-71. Member, UP Legislative Assembly 1952-62 & 1974-77. Lok Sabha 1971-74 and 1977-79 resigned from Congress Party February 1977. General Secretary Congress for Democracy, Feb-May 1977. Member Janata Dal Party 1977-79. Member Fifth Lok Sabha 1971-74. Was union Minister of Communications 1971, Minister of Petroleum and Chemicals and Fertilizers since March, 1977. Finance – 28July – 19 October, 1979.

KALYAN SINGH YADAV
Son of Ch. Tejpal Singh
Small Village Madhauli in Tehsil Atrauli of District Aligarh on January 5, 1932.
B.A.L.T. (Agra University)

He started teaching meanwhile he came in contact with R.S.S. and became its Tehsil Karyavahak. Being influenced by the national leader and renowned Political Thinker Pt. Deendayal Upadhyay, he entered into politics. He was elected member of Vidhan Sabha for seven times so far. He is also a good orater. For the first time elected from Trinli Vidhan Sabha Constituency in 1967 on Jansangh ticket. Later on he was re-elected in 1969, 1974 from the same constituency. After emergency in 1977. He was again elected. Later on, elected for Vidhan Sabha, on BJP Ticket in 1985, 1989 and 1991.

He became Health Minister in Uttar Pradesh Govt. in 1977. He earned honour for his honesty, administrative ability and efficiency. He traveled Thailand, Indonesia and Singapore as a member of the delegation of Health Ministers.

He was elected State General Secretary of BJP in 1980 and State President in 1984.

He went to Jail for seven times for the cause of farmers and labourers. He was imprisoned for 20 months during emergency. He was in Naini Jail for one and half months under NSA during Ram Janam Bhoomi Movement.

Under his leadership, historic rally of 5 lakh Farmers from the state was held in April 1987. Sh. Kalyan Singh is of the view that state will progress if farmers progress.

Elected leader of BJP Vidhan Mandal Party on June 22, 1991, and administered oath of Chief Ministership on June 24, 1991. Former Chief Minister of Uttar Pradesh since September 1997. He was in the news in December 1999 in connection with his explusion from the BJP for 6 years for gross indiscipline and misconduct.

Former U.P. Chief Minister has decided to challenge the Liberhan Commission order issuing a bailable warrant against him for his failure to appear before the Panel on September 2, 2003. The Rashtriya Kranti Party Chief said he had no information about the warrant.

Rashtriya Kranti Party (RKP) will merge with BJP by Febrary 6, 2004 when the Party's National Coucil meet the fomal process of revoking the suspension order against Singh on 3 February, 2004.

Kalyan ends four years 'exile' Prime Minister Vajpayee and BJP General Secretary Pramod Mahajan welcome Klyan Singh to the BJP fold in New Delhi.

KAMALA PATI TRIPATHI
Son of Narayan Pati
Aurangabad. Varanasi (UP)
(03 September 1905-8 October 1990)
Shastri, D.Litt.

Congress (I) MP from Varanasi, UP, 1980. Working President Congress (I) Party. Journalist &Writer joined Freedom

Movement & was imprisoned several times between 1921 & 1942. Minister for Irrigation & Information, Govt. of UP 1952-57; Home, Education & Information 1957-60; Finance 1962-64. Deputy Chief Minister UP 1969-70; Chief Minister 1971-72. Cabinet Minister for Shipping & Transport – 08 again 14 January – 12 November 1980.

MAYAWATI

Daughter of Prabhu Das and Ram Raji

Delhi, 15 January 1956.

B.A., L.L.B., B.Ed.

It is a flowering of Indian democracy that a Dalit women from a village of Ghaziabad (Badalpur Village) has the distinction of becoming a Chief Minister of Uttar Pradesh, the largest state of India.

From her youth time she saw a light of exploited class and vowed to raised the status of Scheduled Castes, minority community. She joined active politics in 1984. Under the influence of Sh. Kanshi Ram on BSP ticket elected to Lok Sabha in 1985 and again in 1986 and elected from Bijanour constituency and in 1994 elected to Uttar Pradesh Council. She became Chief Minister of U.P. in 1995 again in March 1997 and in February 2002 elected to Legislative Assembly UP from Harora, Saharanpur. She has devoted her life for the upliftment of Scheduled Castes and Backward Classes. She established as Chief Minister of U.P. Ambedkar Park and Parvartan Chownk at Lucknow elected to lok Sabha 1989, 1998, 1999, elected to Rajya Sabha 1994-96. She was Chief Minister (1) 3.6.1995 to 17.10.1995 (2) 21.3.1997 to 21.9.1997 (3) 3.5.2002 to August, 2003. Leader of BSP Parliamentary Party, Political Worker, Laywer. She has been re-elected Chief Minister in 2007.

- 13-A, Mall Avenue, Lucknow – 226 001 (UP).

MULAYAM SINGH YADAV
Son of Sulghar Singh
Safayee Village, Etawah District (UP),
21 November, 1939.
M.A., B.T.

Teacher by Profession became President of UP Lok Dal-B after the formation Janata Dal, became President of its UP Unit;. elected to Assembly 1967, 1974, 1977, 1989, 1991; Chief Minister of Uttar Pradesh 1989-91, December 1993-May 1995; Cabinet Minister of Defence – 01 June 1996 to 1 – March 1998, elected to Lok Sabha 1996, 1998, 2002.

Affectionately called "Netaji" 63 year old Mulaym Singh Yadav is poised to return as Chief of Uttar Pradesh for the third time. His first stint as Chief Minister was between 1989 and 1991. His government fell when the BJP withdrew support after he ordered the firing on Kar Sevaks in Ayodhya. He was Chief minister again between 1993 and 1995. When he formed an alliance with Mayawati's BSP. Today, the two are sworn enemies. He was the Union Defence Minister between 1996 to 1998. A follower of Charan Singh and Ram Manohar Lohia, Mulayam has espoused the socialist cause. Known for his strong stand against the demolition of the Babri Masjid. He has been an ardent champion of Minorities. The Former Wrestler and School Teacher has also been a militant Mandalite. He is married to Samantami Yadav. He has one son, Akhilesh who is also a member of Lok Sabha. At present he is Chief Minister of U.P. from 29-08-2003 to till date.
- 5, Vikramaditya Marg, Lucknow (U.P.)

NARAYAN DUTT TIWARI
Son of Poornand Tiwari
Baluti Village, Nainital District (Uttranchal) 18 October 1925.
M.A., L.L.B.

Politician (1) Chief Minister of Uttar Pradesh 1976-77 (2) He was Chief Minister of Uttar Pradesh, 1984-85. Member UP Legislative Assembly 1957-62 & 1969-80. Deputy Leader of the opposition, UP Legislative Assembly 1957-62. Leader of the opposition 1977-79. Leader of Youth Congress delegation of

USSR, 1966. He served the nation with Cabinet Minister for Planning Industry, Labour, Steel & Mines, Industry & Company Affairs during 1980-1985. External Affairs – 22 October 1986 – 25 July 1987. Finance 25 July 1987 – 24 June 1988. Chief Minister of Uttar Pradesh June 1988 – November 1989. At present Chief Minister of Uttaranchal won the Ramnagar Assembly seat on 12 August 2002 defeating his nearest BJP rival Ram Singh Bisht with a margin of nearly 23,000 votes. Ramnagar byelection was necessitated after the ruling party MLA Yogendra Singh Rawat resigned in June last year.
- Ganj Mohalla, Kashipur, Udhan Singh Nagar District, Uttaranchal.

RAJNATH SINGH
Son of Ram Badan Singh
Bhabhaura, P.O. Chakia, Varanasi Dist. (Uttar Pradesh)
10 July 1951.
M.Sc.

In U.P. Rajnath Singh (Union Surface Transport Minister) to replace R.P. Gupta as chief Minister on 25 October 2000 – 27 October 2000. Organising Secretary of ABVP of Gorakhpur Division 1969-71, appointed Secretary Bharatiya jana Sangh, Mirzapur Unit 1974, appointed District president 1975, imprisoned during Emergency 1975-77, elected to Legislative assembly from Mirzapur 1977, was made state BJP Secretary 1983. President State BJP Youth Wing 1984, was member U.P. Legislative Council 1988-94 and also elevated as a member of BJP National Executive was appointed Education Minister of U.P. Govt. 1991; elected to Rajya Sabha 1994 was appointed UP State BJP President on 25 March 1997; re-elected to Rajya Sabha, May 2000. Chief Minister of Uttar Pradesh 28-10-2000 to 08-03-2002.

RAM NARESH YADAV
Son of Gaya Prasad
Anandhipur district, Azamgarh (UP) July 1928.
M.A. L.L.B.

Took part in various movements & agitations and jailed a number of times associated with SP, PSP, SSP, BKD, Janata Party, Lok Dal Samta Party, established educational Institutions, was President Samta party, was General Secretary, Lok Sabha 1977-79, National Executive Janata Party 1977, UP Assembly 1978-85. Chief Minister UP 1977-79. Deputy Chief Minister 1979-80 elected to Rajya Sabha 1988.

- Mohalla Alval, Azamgarh (UP).

RAM PRAKASH GUPTA

26 October, 1923 to 1st May 2004.

M.Sc. (Allahabad University)

Sh. Ram Prakash Gupta sowrn in as Chief Minister of Uttar Pradesh on 12.11.1999 to 28.10.2000.

SMPURNAND (DR.)

January 1, 1891.

B.Sc. L.T. Queen's College Benares.

After graduating worked as a Teacher. Head master Dungar college, Bikaner 1918-21; was Editor, Today (Englesh Daily now defunet) and Maryada (Hindi Monthly). Member A.I.C.C., since 1922. Secretary Thrice U.P. Provincial congress committee. President, second All India socialist conference Bombay; President 29th Hindi Sahitya sammelan, Poona session, 1940. Minister of Education, U.P. Govt. 1938-39. Minister of Education, Finance and Labour, U.P. 1946-51; Home and Labour minister U.P. 1951-54. He was Chief Minister of Uttar Pradesh 28-12-1954 to 06-12-1960.

Publication : 35 Books in Hindi and Sanskrit. Received Mangala Prasad Prize of Rs 1, 200 for his books.

SRIPATI MISHRA

Sultanpur, UP, 20 January 1924-7 December, 2002 .

M.A., L.L.B.

Politician, Member Lok Sabha since 1984. Former Chief Minister of Uttar Pradesh' 1982-84. Entered Govt. Service as Judicial Magistrate, 1954 Resigned in 1958 & joined Congress. Elected to UP Assembly 1962 & 1967. Joined Bharatiya Kranti Dal 1967. Deputy Speaker, UP Assembly 1967. Elected to Lok Sabha 1969, became MLC 1970 & appointed Minister in BKD joined Congress 1971, coalition Govt. of UP Quit BKD & joined congress 1971. Re-elected to UP Assembly 1980 & became Speaker. Attended 26th & 27th Commonwealth Parliamentary

Conference at Lusaka & Suva in 1980,1981 & 1987 respectively.
- Toder Mal Lane, New Delhi – 110011.

SUCHETA KRIPALANI
Ambala (Punjab) June, 1908.
Married Acharya J.B. Kripalani, was Professor of Constitutional History, Banaras Hindu University.
M.A. (Delhi University)

Secretary Women's Section, Indian National Congress and its for its foreign department and one and a half years; Imprisoned for participating in Congress Movements, 1940 and 1944.

Indian Freedom Fighter and first woman Chief Minister of Independent India (UP), 1963-67. Appointed organizing Secretary Kasturba Memorial Trust 1945, returned to Parliament from Gonda Constituency, UP, February 1967. Member, Working Committee A.I.C.C., 1947, Board of Trustes Gandhi National memorial Trust 1945-47. U.P. Legislative Assembly 1948-50. First Lok Sabha 1952-56 and second Lok Sabha 1957-62. Leader of the Parliamentary Delegation to Turkey in November, 1954.

TRIBHUVAN NARAYAN SINGH
Son of Prasidh Narayan Singh
Varanasi, 08 August 1904-3 August, 1982.
Shastri
He was Secretary Lal Bahadur Shastri National Memorial Trust. Chairman Public Accounts Committee 1957-58, 1974-75. Member Planning Commission 1958-67, elected to Rajya Sabha 1974, 1970. Chief Minister of Uttar Pradesh 1970-71.

VIR BAHADUR SINGH

He was Minister of Uttar Pradesh from 24-09-1985 to 24-06-1985.

VISHWANATH PRATAP SINGH
Son of Raja Bahadur Ram Gopal Singh
Allahabad, 25 June 1931.
B.A., L.L.B., B.Sc.

Union Minister for Finance since January 1985. Chief Minister of Uttar Pradesh 1980-82. President, Uttar Pradesh PCC,

September 1984-December 1984. Union Minister of Commerce 1982-84. Congress (I) Member in Lok Sabha from Allahabad, UP 1980. Deputy Minister of Commerce, Govt. India, 1974-76 & Minister of State for Commerce, 1976-77. Member, AICC 1969-71 & UP Assembly, 1969-71. Whip congress Legislative Party, UP 1970 – 71. Member Lok Sabha 1971-77. Prime Minister of India December 1989 – November 1990. President Janata Dal 1988; Convenor National Front – 1988.
- Manda, Allahabad Dist (UP).

CHIEF MINISTERS OF UTTRANCHAL

Sr. No.	Name	Term of Office
1.	Nityanand Swami	
2.	Bhagat Singh Koshiyari	29-10-2001 to 2002
3.	Naryan Dutt Tiwari	2002 to Nov. 2006
4.	B.C. Khanduri	7.11.2006 to Till Date

BHUWAN CHANDRA KHANDURI
S/o Jai Ballabh Khanduri
01 October, 1934 at Dehradun (Uttarakhand)
B.Sc., B.E., M.I.E., (Major General (Retd.))

He was Minister of State for Road Transport and Highways (Independent Charge) – 07 November 2006 – till date

UTTARANCHAL

BHAGAT SINGH KOSHIYARI
Mahagari Kapkot Village in Bageshwar district 1942
M.A.

Shri B.S.. Koshiyari is the Second Chief Minister of the newly-created State of Uttaranchal. He took oath of office on October 29, 2001. Following resignation of the first chief Minister. Mr. Nityanand Swami. He was associated with Prabat Piyush, a Hindi Weekly published from Pithoragarh since 1975. A keen educationist, he has set up many educational institutions at Pithoragarh. Began his career as a Lecturer. This R.S.S. Pracharak took over as Uttaranchal's second chief minister in October, 2001 replacing N. Swami under whom he was a minister for energy, irrigation, law and legislative affairs.

NARAYAN DUTT TIWARI
Son of Poornand Tiwari
Dist. Nainital, 19 October 1925
M.A., L.L.B.

He is the Chief Minister of Uttaranchal won the Ram Nagar assembly seat on 12 August 2002 defeating his nearest BJP rival Ram Singh Bisht by 23,000 votes.

Chief Minister of Uttar Pradesh 1984-85.

Chief Minister of UP, 1976-77. Member U.P. Legislative Assembly 1957-62 & 1969-80. Deputy Leader of the opposition, UP Legislative Assembly, 1957-62, Leader of the Opposition, 1977-79. Leader Youth Congress Delegation to USSR, 1966.

At Present he is Chief Minister of Uttaranchal Pradesh since 2002 till date.

NITYANAND SWAMI

He was First Chief Minister of Uttaranchal Pradesh for sometimes.

CHIEF MINISTERS OF WEST BENGAL

Sr. No.	Name	Term of Office
1.	Dr. Prafulla Chandra Ghosh	August14-15, 1947 to 22.01.1948 (Mid Night)
2.	Dr. B.C. Roy	23.01.1948 to 01.07.1962
3.	P.C. Sen	09.07.1962 to 01.03.1967
4.	Ajay Kumar Mukherjee	02.03.1967 to 28.11.1967
5.	Dr. Prafulla Chandra Ghosh	21.11.1967 to 28.11.1967
6.	President's Rule	20.02.1968 to 24.02.1969
7.	Ajay Kumar Mukherjee	25.02.1969 to 16.03.1970
8.	President's Rule	19.03.1970 to 10.03.1971
9.	Ajay Kumar Mukherjee	02.04.1971 to 25.06.1971
10.	President's Rule	29.07.1971 to 19.03.1972
11.	Sidhartha Shankar Ray	20.03.1972 to 29.04.1977
12.	President's Rule	30.04.1977 to 20.06.1977
13.	Jyoti Basu	21.06.1977 to 10.05.2001
14.	Budhadeb Bhattacharjee	18.05.2001 to till date

WEST BENGAL

AJOY KUMAR MUKHERJEE
Son of Sarat Chandra and Indumati Devi.
Tamluk (W.B) 13 April, 1901.
B.A.

Join Non-Co-Operation Movement, 1921, suffered improsonment several times during freedom movement, was "Supreme Leader" in 'National Govt.' established in Tamlok during Quit India Movement; elected Leader of UF Legislature Party, 1969, Chief Minister of West Bengal
(1) 02.03.1967 to 28.11.1967.
(2) 25.02.1969 to 16.03.1970
(3) 02.04.1971 to 25.06.1971.

BIDHAN CHANDRA RAY
Son of Late Babu Prakash Chandra Ray.
(July 01, 1882-1962)
M.D. M.R.C.P. (London)F.R.C.S (England).
D.S. (Cal & Allababad)

Indian National leader, First Indian to obtain MRCP and FRCS in one calender year. Mayor of Calcutta (1931). Chief Minister of West Bengal 1948-62. Awarded Bharat Ratna 1961.

BUDDHADEV BHATTACHARJEE
Son of Nepal Chandra and Lila
Calcutta, 01 March 1944.
B.A., (Hons.)

Member, Provincial Committee of West Bengal CPI (M); Member Central Committee of the CPI (M). Minister for Information & Cultural Affairs, Local Government since 1987. After Jyoti Basu he became Chief Minister of West Bengal since November 2001 to till date.

JYOTI BASU
Son of Nishikanta & Hemalata
08 July 1914 at Culcutta.
B.A., Bar at-Law.

Chief Minister of West Bengal 1977, Deputy Chief Minister and Minister of Finance and Transport, 1967-68. Dy. Chief Minister and Minister of Home, Member Politbureau, Central Committee and West Bengal State Committee of CPI (M), since 1964. Leader of opposition, WB Assembly 1957-71. Elected to Bengal Legislative Council, 1946. Member West Bengal Assembly since 1947 was member CPI, 1947-67. Member Central Executive Committee CPI (M) has been joined several times. Veteran Communist Leader of India. Chief Minister of West Bengal for a record five consecutive terms i.e., 1977 – 2001. Associated with India League and Federation of Indian Students in England.
- 55-B, Hindustan Park, Calcutta – 700 029.

PRAFULLA CHANDRA SEN
Village of Sahabad District, Bihar 1897.
B.Sc.

Was articled to a firm of incorporated Accountants. Joined the Non-Cooperation Movement and went to Hoogly district as a teacher. Hoogly Vidyamandir, took a leading part in the Mass Civil Disobedience Movements organized in the years 1930, 1932 and 1942 in Arambagh. Sub-division to Hoogly Dist.; courted jail several times, elected MLA West Bengal on Congress ticket from Khanakul constituency with an overwhelming majority 1962. Chief Minister, West Bengal July 9, 1962-67.

SIDDHARTHA SHANKAR RAY
Son of Sudhir Chandra Ray & Aparna Devi.
Calcutta (West Bengal) 20 October 1920.
B.A., L.L.B. Bar-at-Law.

Cabinet Minister for Education, Culture & Social Welfare – 18 March 1971 – 20 March 1972. Chief Minister of West Bengal 1972-77. Chairman Civil Rights Committee, AICC, 1986. North Zone Cultural Centre 1986. (1) Governor of Punjab, April 2, 1986 – December 7, 1989 (2) Ambassor to U.S. 1992. President

West Bengal PCC 1991-92. Cricket Association of Bengal 1982-92. President West Bengal PCC 1991-92. Cricket Association of Bengal 1982-86.

- 2 Beitala Road, Calcutta – 700 026.
- 1/19, Shanti Niketan, New Delhi.

UNION TERRITORIES

ANDAMAN & NICOBAR
CHIEF SECRETARY

ANIL BAIJAL

He was Chief Secretary of Andaman & Nicobar Islands.

R. PADMANABHAN, (Dr.)

Dr. R. Padmanabhan is Lt. Governor of Andaman and Nicobar Islands.

CHANDIGARH

TRILOKI NATH CHATURVEDI
S/o Pt. Kamal Nath Chaturvedi
Tirwa, Distt (U.P.), 18 January, 1928.
M.A., LL.B., Visharad.

Joined I.A.S. in 1950. He was Joint Director, National Academy of Administration Mussoori 1967-71. Chief Commissioner, Chandigarh, 1976-78.

Director Indian Institute of Public Administration. At present he is chairman Nehru Memorial Museum & Library, Teen Murti, New Delhi.

Presently Governor of Karanataka.

DADRA AND NAGAR HAVELI

DAMAN AND DIU

CHIEF MINISTERS OF DELHI (NCT)

S. No.	Name	Term of Office	
1.	Brahm Prakash Chowdhury	1952	1955
2.	Mushtaq Ahmad Mir	1966	1967
3.	Vijay Kumar Malhotra	1967	1972
4.	Madan Lal Khurana	1977	1980
5.	Jag Parvesh Chandra	1983	1990
6.	Dr. Sahib Singh Verma	1996	Oct. 1998
7.	Sushma Swaraj	Oct. 1998	2000
8.	Radha Raman		
9.	Sheila Dikshit	1998	Till date

DELHI

BRAHM PRAKASH CHOWDHURY
Son of Bhagwan Das & Parvati
Nairobi (Kenya) 16 June 1918.

President, Delhi P.C.C. 1951-52, 1966-67. Chief Minister Delhi State 1952-55; Member Lok Sabha 1957-70 & 1977-79; Chairman Bharatiya Kisan Union. General Secretary NCUI 1962-70. Minister for Agriculture & Irrigation GoI 1979-80; participated in freedom movement & imprisoned four times during 1941-45. Also imprisoned during emergency; President National Union of Backward classes; SC & ST Minorities.
- A 6/3, Vasant Vihar, New Delhi-57.

JAG PARVESH CHANDRA (Chief Executive Councilor)
Son of Sh. K.C. Talwar.
Gujaranwala in Pakistan, 12 November 1916 — 21 February 2002.
Journalist, B.A., LL.B.

An outstanding Political Personality known for his honesty, integrity and straight forwardness. Member of Delhi Assembly in 1952. He became chief executive councilor from 1983 to 1990. and finally leader of the opposition from 1993-1998. He opted out of the 1998 Assembly Polls on health grounds. He was also the chairman as well as Vice-Chairman in the Metropolitan council. He was secretary of the All India student Federation at government college Lahore.

The grand oldman of Delhi Politics, was keeping indifferent health for some time. He was 89. Shri Chandra was in fact the first leader to start the clean Delhi – Green Delhi campaign during his time as chief executive councellor published 49 books. Participated in Quit India Movement 1942.

MADAN LAL KHURANA
Son of S.D. Khurana
Lyallpur (Pakistan) 15 October 1936.
M.A., B.Ed.

Started his career as school teacher member Interim Metropolitan Council, Metro-council 1967-89, Executive Councillor 1977-80; elected to Lok Sabha 1989, 1991, 1998 Delhi Cabinet Minister for Parliamentary Affairs, & Tourism 19 March 1998 – 30 January 1999.

He has contested 12 elections from Delhi. won 11, only lost in 1984, when no BJP candidate won. Shri Madan Lal Khurana sworn as Delhi's first Chief Minister.

In November 1993, resigned after Howala Scandal in February 1996. As BJP in-charge of Haryana and Punjab, worked out allience with Akali Dal and INLD in 1998–99.

He was brought back to Delhi Politics in 2003 and made Chairman of Delhi Metro Rail Carporation.

He was Rajasthan Governor.

- 104, Kirti Nagar, New Delhi.

MUSHTAQ AHMAD MIR (Chief Executive Councilor)
Son of Mir Abdul Sattar.
Shimla (H.P.), 25 April 1975.
B.A .

He was teacher, Ramjas school 1940, took part in individual Stayagraha, 1940, detained during Quit India Movement, 1942; special Magistrate, 1947; Member Delhi Assembly, 1952; President Delhi Pradesh Congress committee, 1963-66; chief executive councillar, Delhi, 1966; chairman, Metropolitan council of Delhi, 1972-77.

RADHA RAMAN

Radha Raman was born at Delhi on August 4th 1904. Joined the Indian National Congress & associated with leaders like Gandhiji, Pt. Nehru, Subhash Chandra, Patel & others. He represented the people of Delhi in the first two Parliaments, and was ultimately chosen as the Chief Executive Councillor (e.g. to C.M.) of Delhi. He was Chief Minister of Delhi.

DR. SAHIB SINGH VERMA
Delhi, 15 March 1943.
Ph.D., M.A. (Eco.), M.Lib.Sc.

He was member Municipal Corporation of Delhi 1977 & 1983. Deputy Leader of opposition in M.C.D. 1993, elected to Delhi Assembly 1993. Development Minister Govt. of Delhi 1993 – February 1996. Chief Minister of Delhi, Government of Delhi February 1996 – October 1998. He was Labour Minister in the Union Cabinet of India during NDA Government.

SHEILA DIKSHIT (Mrs.)
Daughter of Shri Krishna Kapoor
Kapurthala (Punjab) 31 March 1938.
M.A.

Married Vinod Kumar Dikshit (I.A.S.), Elected to Lok Sabha 1984, Minister of State for Parliamentary Affairs – 12 May 1986 – 02 December 1989. Prime Minister's Office – 25 June 1988 – 2 December 1989. Government of India nominee on the UN Commission on Status of Women, since 1984. President Delhi Pradesh Congress Committee. Chief Minister of Delhi, Delhi Assembly 1998 to till date. Delhi government's Citizen-government Partnership Programme Bhagidari has won the 2005 UN Public Service Award.

- 3-b-4, L.D.A. Flats, Park Road, Hazartgaj, Lucknow (UP).

SUSHMA SWARAJ (Mrs.)
Daughter of Hardev Sharma
Ambala Cantt (Haryana) 14 February 1952.
Married : Swaraj Kaushal.
B.A., L.L.B.

Knows German and Sanskrit State President Hindi Sahitya Sammelan 1978-82; President Haryana State Janata Party 1981-83; Minister in Devi Lal Govt. 1977-1978. Secretary All India BJP; elected to Rajya Sabha 1990 to Lok Sabha, 1996, 1998. cabinet Minister for Information & Broadcasting – 16 May - 01 June 1996, again 19 March – 11 October 1998. Communications – 20 April – 11 October 1998. Information & Broadcasting – 30 September 2000 She was the first woman Chief Minister of Delhi 12 October 1998 – replacing Shri Sahib Singh Verma.

- House No. 667, Sector 8, Chandigarh.
- 8 Tees January Marg, New Delhi – 110 011.

VIJAY KUMAR MALHOTRA (Chief Executive Councilor)
Son of Shri. Khazan Chandra and Sushila.
Lahore, (Pakistan) 3 December 1931.
M.A., Ph.D.

He was Secretary Bharatiya Janata Party and member Rajya Sabha began career as Journalist, He was with Veer Arjun and Akashvani 1950-54. member of Jansang; President of Delhi unit 1973-77, member of Delhi Municipal corporation 1958-62; 1962-67; member Delhi Metropolitan council 1967-77; chief executive councilor Delhi 1967-72, Member Lok Sabha 1977-79, re-elected 1989.

In 1953 when the Jan sangh started the Kashmir Movement with Dr. S. Mukerjee as leader, Malhotra gave momentum to the movement in Delhi and was jailed for eight months. He became teacher in DAV college. President Archery Association of India 1973-76. Asian Games Delhi 1979. Delhi olympics Association, Chief-de-mission of Indian contingent to Asian Games 1974, commonwealth games 1978; Vice-President, Indian Olympic Association. President, General Association of National Sports Federation (India). He was one of the founders of Delhi university students union (DUSU) and became its first secretary. Presently Spoken Person, BJP, Member Lok Sabha
6, Dr. Bishambhar Das Marg, New Delhi – 110001
T.No. 23715051

CHIEF MINISTERS PONDICHERRY

S. No.	Name	Term of Office	
1.	V.Venkatasubba Reddiar.	11 Sept, 1964	1967
2.	M.O.H. Farook	1967	1968
3.	M.O.H. Farook	1969	1974
4.	S. Rama Swamy	1974	1979
5.	D. Ramachandran	1980	1984
6.	V.V. Vaithilingam	1993	1994
7.	N. Rangaswamy	2000	2003
8.	M.M. Lakhera	2003	Tiil date

PONDICHERRY

Pondicherry, according to a legend, was once called "Vedapuri" a seat of learning and Vedic Culture, and was an abode of Sage Agastya. According to a French archaeologist, the main building of Aurobindo Ashram Stands where Agastya had his Ashram.

Pondicherry was a French Colony for 281 years till 1954 and carried indelible marks of a rich Cultural and architectural heritage : Mother" a Paris born Painter and Musician, and a close companian of Shri Aurobindo, was instrumental in setting up the ashram which is now one of the Landmarks.

Pondicherry became a Union Terriroty in 1954 when Pandit Jawaharlal Nehru Memorial Museum and Library accorded a special status to Pondicherry to preserved it as a link between the French and Indian Cultures.

D. RAMACHANDRAN
Son of Deivanayaga Reddiar & Singaram
Maducarai (Pondicherry) 31 January 1934.
Intermediate.

Took active interest in Co-operative movement; Member Pondicherry Assembly 1969; Minister for Public Works, 1969-74, for Industries and Education, 1974 for Home, Transport, Agriculture, Public Works & Electricity, 1977-78; Chief Minister 1980-84.
- Labour-donnais St., Pondicherry.

M.M. LAKHERA. Lt. General (Retd.)
The Lieutenant Governor (LG) of Pondicherry has expressed his gratitude to the UPA Governments for setting up a separate department of Ex-serviceman welfare in Defence Ministry.

M.O.H. FAROOQ
Son of Hasan Kuthoos
Karaikal (Pondicherry), 06 September 1937.
B.A.

Politician, Chief Minister of pondicherry 1967-68; 1969-74.

Took active part in the anti-merger agitation (Pondicherry with Tamil Nadu) and jailed, 1979. Member and Leader of Congress Party. First elected MLA Pondicherry 1964.

Member Pondicherry 1964, 1967, 1980, 1985; Speaker 1964-67, 1980-85. Chief Minister 1967-68, 1969-74, 1985-90; resigned and joined DMK, leader of opposition 1990, elected to Lok Sabha 1991; Minister of State for Civil Aviation and Tourism – 21 June 1991 – 02 July 1992. Civil Aviation – 02 July 1992 – 17 January 1993. Joined DMK, from Calapeth, March 1969.

- 64, Saffron Street, Pondicherry.

N. RANGASAMY

Son of Thiru Nadesan Krishnasamy and Smt. Panchali.

Thelarshpet, Pondicherry, August 4, 1950

B.Com., B.L.A. (Congress-I).

In the Ever First Election contesed in 1990, he has defeated in the Thattanchavady Constituency. Later he was chosen in 1991 Election with a overwhelming majority and was appointed as Minister for Agriculture & Co-operation. Again elected in the same constituency in 1996 and during 2000 he had resumed the office of the minister for Tourism dealt with Education, public Health Engineering, Civil Aviation, Art & Culture and Govt. Automobile Workshop. In the recent election held in 2001 he was elected with highest margin in the Union Territory of Pondicherry and appointed as Minister for Public Works, Agriculture, Forests, public Health Engineering and Govt. Automobile Workshop. In the same year he was selected for the Highest Post of Chief Minister and continuing his selfless service.

He paid keen interest in helping the proletarian groups. Interested in driving Motorcycle. Mingling with General public on all occasions. In his extra curriculum, he plays Badminton, Football & Kabaddi. He was Chief Minister 2000 till date.

- No 9, Vinayagar Koli Street,Thelarshpet, Pondicherry-605 009.
Ph. : 0413-333399, 335530, 335522m 335328

S. RAMASWAMY
Son of R,Subramaniam & Pattammal
05 June 1939.
B.Sc., B.L.

Member Pondicherry Assembly, 1969-74. Chief Minister 1977-79.

- 8, Veerasamy Maicker St. Karaikal.

V. VENKATASUBBA REDDIAR
December 18, 1909.
B.A.

Municipal Councillor for Nettapakkam Commune, 1944-45; Mayour Nettapakka, 1945-64; M.L.A. Pondicherry since 1955; President Pondicherry State Congress 1958-60. Leader Pondicherry State Legislature Assembly & Chief Councillor 1953-64' took active part in the anti-merger movement, Pondicherry with T.N.was leading member French India Liberation Govt. He is an ordent follower of Gandhian Principles; Minister for Development, Pondicherry, July 1963 – September 1964. Chief Minister, Pondicherry since September 11, 1964 to 1967.

V.V. VAITHININGAM
He is Chief Minister of pondicherry 1993-94.

APPENDIX-1

Women Chief Minister of India

S. No.	Name	State	Period	Party
1.	Sucheta Kripalani	Uttar Pradesh	Oct. 1963-March 1967	Congress
2.	Nandini Satpaty	Orissa	June 1972-March 74 & March 74 – December 1976	Congress
3.	Shashikala Khodokar	Goa	August 1973-june 77 & June 77 – April 1979.	Maharashtr a Gomantak Party
4.	Syeda Anwara Taimur	Assam	Dec. 1980 – June 1981	Congress
5.	Janaki Ramachandran	Tamil Nadu	Jan.7, 1980-1988	ADMK (Janaki)
6.	J. Jayalalitha	Tamil Nadu	June 1991 – May 1996	ADMK
7.	Mayawati	Uttar Pradesh	June 1995-oct. 1996 & March 1997 – Sept. 1997	BSP
8.	Rajinder Kaur Bhattal	Punjab	April 1996-Feb. 1997	Congress
9.	Rabri Devi	Bihar	July 25, 1997-Feb. 1999 & April 99-March 2000 & 11 March 2000	RJD
10.	Sushma Swaraj	Delhi	12 Oct. 98 – 3 December 98	BJP
11.	Sheila Dixit	Delhi	Since December 3, 1998.	Congress
12.	Vasundhara Raje Scindia	Rajasthan	In 2003	BJP
13.	Uma Bharati	M.P.	Since 2003	BJP

CHIEF MINISTER'S ROLL CALL

Buddhadeb Bhattacharjee (59), B.A. from Presidency.
J. Jayalalitha (55), Matric
Mayawati (47), LLB, B.Ed.
N. Chandrababu Naidu (51), MA Economics.
Narendra Modi (52), MA in Political Science.
Rabri Devi (46) Class IV pass.
S. M. Krishna (71), Masters in Civil Law from Texas.
Sushilkumar Shinde (62), L.L.B.
Uma Bharti Class VI Pass

LLBS GALORE

39 TN MLAs are LLBs.
UP has at least three LLB ministers, Andhra and Karnataka have two each.
Maharashtra has four.

ONLY SCHOOL

31 MLAs in Tamil Nadu are below Matric level. The lowest being four members, only 5th pass.
The least qualified MLA in Gujarat is Class VII pass.
In Karnataka, nine ML/As are below SSLC.
West Bengal's Assembly has 28 non-matrics.
In UP 100 have not furnished details of their educational qualification.
Among those who have, six are non-matriculate.
In Maharashtra 19 have not made it to Class X, while 62 MLAs are SSC pass.
Bashir Moosa Patil of NCP says he has a diploma in plumbing.
In M.P. Uma Bharati was under matric.

YOUNG TURKS

Tamil Nadu has 96 MLAs below 45 years.
In Uttar Pradesh, average age of MLAs is 42.

INDEX